Praise

"Marjorie's reflections describe her unique ability to improve the lives of others—a skill not limited to only those she has raised. I have had the privilege of joining Marjorie on her journey to train women around the world to become 'participants' in their own futures. She has unequivocally made a difference in the lives of thousands of women around the world."

VALERIE BIDEN OWENS

"Marjorie's vote not only had huge positive consequences for our nation but was also the most courageous vote I've ever seen. People in America want leaders willing to vote for principles over politics. That's exactly what they got with Marjorie—someone who knowingly put her political career in jeopardy to do not what was easy but what was right. She stood up and did what Americans from all across the country, from every region and political party, want in their leaders: an authentic person showing personal and political courage."

JOE KENNEDY II,
FORMER CONGRESSMAN (D) MASSACHUSETTS

"She [Margolies] had earned an honored place in history, with a vote she shouldn't have had to cast."

PRESIDENT BILL CLINTON

"I consider my mother a saint. She raised four boys. Marjorie Margolies raised eleven children, two she adopted before she had a husband, four she inherited through marriage, two she gave birth to, and three were part of her Vietnamese family that lived with her for 23 years. When you finish reading *And How Are the Children?* you may wish she had raised you."

CHRISTOPHER SHAYS,
FORMER CONGRESSMAN (R) CONNECTICUT

"Who would think world peace depended on *And How Are the Children?* Well, when you hear what Marjorie Margolies has done during and after raising eleven children you will agree. She knows how to start an important conversation that leads to a solution. As a proud father of eight I can agree with her 73%! Oh, by the way, how *are* the kids?"

RICHARD N. SWETT, FAIA,
FORMER CONGRESSMAN (D) NEW HAMPSHIRE,
AMBASSADOR AND CURRENT ARCHITECT, AUTHOR OF
LEADERSHIP BY DESIGN: CREATING AN ARCHITECTURE OF TRUST

"Marjorie captures the fun, chaos and joy of eleven children in one family! She reminds me of my experience as the eldest of eleven. This may not be for everyone but it sure is a blast!"

KATHLEEN KENNEDY TOWNSEND,
FORMER LT. GOVERNOR OF MARYLAND

"'A visionary,' 'fearless,' 'a trailblazer' are just some of the words I would use to describe Marjorie's tireless and revolutionary work in the advocation, promotion and empowerment of millions of women across the world. Marjorie's brilliantly pioneering work in Malawi included educating women on HIV/AIDS, legal advocacy and reducing adolescent pregnancy. Marjorie is a woman of courage, generosity, and immeasurable compassion, and it is an honour to be able to call her my friend."

CALLISTA JENNIE MUTHARIKA (CHIMOMBO),
FORMER FIRST LADY OF THE REPUBLIC OF MALAWI

"*And How Are the Children* is a book full of warmth and wisdom, and of unforgettable stories of the author's amazing life and times. I could not put it down. The story of Marjorie Margolies is one of the most remarkable of our era—it is a story of a nationally prominent journalist, of a teacher and writer, of a Congresswoman and of a mother, step-mother and adoptive mother of eleven children. Marjorie embodies the adage that happiness in an interdependent world—in a world attuned to women's rights—requires that individuals embrace and excel in multiple personal, social and professional roles. How is that done? My favorite maxim in this book is what Marjorie calls the 'twelve-word rule' which simply stated is 'never use more than twelve words to answer the question (of a child).'

What accounts for Marjorie's amazing ability to live life to the maximum? This book provides the answer: 'Marjorie's extraordinary energy, optimism, imagination, intelligence, her love of life and people.' This book is one of the most enjoyable and important books I have read in a decade."

DAVID EISENHOWER,
AUTHOR, PUBLIC POLICY FELLOW,
PROFESSOR AT THE UNIVERSITY OF PENNSYLVANIA

"Marjorie, through anecdote, story, and courage, shares with the reader an amazing journey of individual resilience, great success, and deep sadness. All can learn about the enduring family through her openness and honesty."

STEPHEN TREAT,
FORMER DIRECTOR AND CEO OF
COUNCIL FOR RELATIONSHIPS

And How Are the Children?

Also by Marjorie Margolies

A WOMAN'S PLACE (1994)
THE "GIRLS" IN THE NEWSROOM (1983)
FINDING SOMEONE TO LOVE (1980)
THEY CAME TO STAY (1976)

And How Are the Children?

Timeless Lessons from the Frontlines of Motherhood

*After Raising a Family of Adopted, Homegrown,
Step, and Sponsored Kids*

MARJORIE MARGOLIES

Wyatt-MacKenzie Publishing
DEADWOOD, OREGON

And How Are the Children?

Timeless Lessons from the Frontlines of Motherhood
After Raising a Family of Adopted, Homegrown, Step, and Sponsored Kids

Marjorie Margolies

Library Hardcover ISBN: 978-1-954332-15-7
Hardcover ISBN: 978-1-954332-35-5
Softcover ISBN: 978-1-954332-29-4
Ebook ISBN: 978-1-954332-30-0

Library of Congress Control Number: 2021946785

Cover photos are from author's personal collection.
View more photos at MarjorieMargolies.com.

The poem "The Answer (To an Adopted Child)" by Fleur Conkling Heyliger
on page 31 is reprinted with permission from *The Saturday Evening Post*
© 1952 The Curtis Publishing Company.

Wyatt-MacKenzie Publishing
DEADWOOD, OREGON

www.WyattMacKenzie.com

Dedication

TO MY PARENTS Herbert and Mildred who always allowed me to express myself and take chances. They were quite remarkable, as you will learn in this book. My dad (Pop-pop) was hilarious, and his love of carrots earned him the nickname Herbert the Hare. My mother was a celebrated artist who put her family first, often with orange-tinged hands as she prepared my father's favorite food.

In addition to these amazing parents, I'd like to dedicate this book to my grandchildren: Lucas, Ryan, Griffin, Jude, Trent, Sebastian, Dexter, Isla, Charlotte, Aidan, Jasper, Serena, Gabriel, Daniel, Alexander, Ethan, Juliette, Mimi, Lucas, Hailey, and Charlie.

Contents

PART III
Reflections

The Masai tribe of Africa comprises renowned warriors who
have been celebrated for their bravery and intelligence for
centuries. Their traditional greeting to each other is not
"How are you?"; it's "Kasserian Ingera," which means,
"And how are the children?"

That Masai tradition continues to this day.
When asked that question, the usual answer is,
"The children are well."

Foreword
by Hillary Rodham Clinton

I'VE KNOWN MARJORIE MARGOLIES as a Member of Congress, brave lawmaker, founder of Women's Campaign International, advocate for women's rights at home and abroad, mother, and grandmother. It is her role as a mother of adopted, step, and biological children that she describes and explores in this book. And what a story it is!

As a single woman television journalist, she decided to adopt a little girl in South Korea who had won her heart. That little girl was followed by another girl from Vietnam and they were later joined by nine others, parented by Marjorie and her husband at that time.

As the mother of one child, I'm awed by Marjorie's gumption and creativity as she navigates the varying demands of babies, toddlers, and teenagers all at the same time. She tells their and her stories with humor, empathy, and self-deprecation. If you've ever been a parent or a child (which I think covers everybody) you'll find something to make you laugh, cry, or shake your head in recognition as Marjorie recounts her mothering journey.

And, how do I know her as a grandmother? That's easy. Her son, Marc, is married to my daughter, Chelsea, and we share the joys of three exceptional grandchildren.

PART I

Building a Family

I REALLY BELIEVE THAT GIVING BIRTH is only a small part of motherhood and certainly not a requirement. Mothering is caring. It's nurturing and holding a child lightly until you let that child go. Caring means giving your children the strength so they can enter life and fulfill their potential.

When I look at my children, I think, "They are only mine for a short time. The day will come when they will leave." Mothering means letting go and watching your children as they *become*—happily, sadly. But we never completely let go; we just switch gears and become sensitive to their lives.

CHAPTER 1

Losing a Country, Finding a Family

Look at life with the eyes of a child.

– KATHE KOLLWITZ, GERMAN ARTIST

MY NAME IS VU LINH PHAM. It still amazes me to think I came over on a boat with my mom. In 1979, we escaped from our native land, leaving behind my father and our life in Vietnam. Once in America, we moved in with the Margolies-Mezvinsky family. Then, in 2010, I found myself giving the "best man" speech at Marc Mezvinsky and Chelsea Clinton's wedding.

Now, when I look at pictures of parents clinging to their children while attempting to cross the southern US border, I'm reminded of my mother jumping into the South China Sea with me tied to her back after fleeing Vietnam. I was one of those "boat people" who had fled his native land as the United States withdrew after the Communist North Vietnamese Army sacked the presidential palace in Saigon.

The nuances of immigration policy are far more complex than the simple binary views espoused by many to serve their own interests. I do not have policy remedies for this complex issue, nor do I add my support to one side of this contentious debate, but merely wish to tell my story of immigrating to the United States on a boat when I was four years old.

Many people believe immigrants will not pay their fair share of taxes, or that they bring in diseases such as COVID and commit crimes. These fear-mongering narratives are not based in fact but are fed by media outlets which rarely focus on the basic reasons people risk their lives to leave their countries.

My biological father Minh Duong Pham was imprisoned by the North Vietnamese communists for simply being on the losing side after the war. All opposers were punished. I remember my mother telling me what happened to those unable to leave Vietnam after its fall. Victorious soldiers entered her friend's house and said the home was no longer hers. It was now the property of the people of Vietnam. One soldier ripped out earrings from her bloodied ears and proclaimed, "these earrings too now belong to the people of Vietnam." Common theft in the name of nationalistic communism. Her bank accounts and assets were seized by the new government in the name of the people. The next day soldiers moved into her home with their families.

My mother's choice was not to stay, with dim economic prospects coupled with a constant fear of physical retaliation as befell her friend or risk a dangerous escape from Vietnam on a fishing boat. She paid Chinese smugglers 14 troy ounces of gold for a one-way adult ticket and six ounces for my junior ticket. There was no Costco return policy or fine print for those tickets. It is estimated that 200,000 to 400,000 lives were lost at sea as Vietnamese fled the soil of their ancestors to begin anew on distant shores.

I remember the captain of the vessel giving my mother a tranquilizer laced in the iconic Coca Cola soda to silence me as I was screaming to be released as we hid in the cramped hull surrounded by other escaping families. She told the captain she gave me the Coca Cola as she spilled the potentially lethal elixir over her shoulder. She overheard the captain say the increased dose was enough to silence an elephant. (Funny thing is, today I am an anesthesiologist who injects drugs to put people asleep. I depress the plunger more quickly if the conversation isn't going well or they don't laugh at my pre-surgery standup routine.) We were boarded by Thai pirates who demanded valuables lest they sink the boat. My mother had sewn cash into the leaves of her straw hat and managed to hide it from them. Many young daughters were raped and forced to leave with the pirates, never to see their parents again. The ones that were returned to our vessel came back with vacant stares.

Upon reaching the Malaysian waters, the Chinese smugglers forced everyone off the boat to swim the remaining 100 yards. My mother, who never learned how to swim, stubbornly demanded a flotation device. She tied me tightly to her body with two pairs of pants. They finally relented to her iron stubbornness and gave her a tire. Exhausted after battling the waves to reach the beach, my mother looked over to hear the sobs of my cousin. Her young child lay lifeless on the sand. He had aspirated too much seawater during the swim.

We survived for six months at the Palau Bidong camp with the help of humanitarian groups. We hunted for crabs as well as sympathetic soldiers who would give us candy and cartons of milk to supplement the rations provided by the international aid groups. (The camp would swell to 40,000 refugees at its peak until the last refugee left in 1991.)

Whether by divine intervention or an extra flap of a butterfly's wings, my "sponsor" file landed on the desk of one of the social workers of the Lutheran Refugee and Immigration

Service. They placed my mother and me with a family that was blended and diverse before it was fashionable. It was a Jewish American family residing in the Philadelphia suburbs.

My new "American father" had four girls from a previous marriage and my "American mother" had first adopted a Korean girl and then a Vietnamese-Caucasian girl when she was still single. The couple then had two biological sons together. These Vietnamese, Korean, Catholic, Jewish, conservative, and progressive worlds coalesced to create an unforgettable childhood. Those people became my sisters and my brothers and my mother and my father. They became my family.

I remember that my biological mom literally prayed that I would become a priest. She's a devout Catholic, and my biological father was going to become a priest also, but that didn't quite pan out. One day, after she'd brought up the topic again, I told Marjorie, "I don't want to become a priest. I'm going to have a bar mitzvah like everyone else." I went as far as saying the blessing for bread at Seder. I'm sure it was interesting to see this Vietnamese teenager reciting Jewish prayers.

I straddled two worlds. My biological mom Suu Thi Vu was a pious, strict woman who possessed a traditional, old-school world view. I remember my friend and I would sneak girls into the house when we were in seventh grade. It was perfectly innocent because we were just talking and laughing. Marjorie, my American mom, would be in cahoots and help us hide them from my biological mom who would have forbade my actions as inappropriate. I could seek the advice of one mom for one issue and the other one for another issue.

I had fun with it and there was never any conflict or drama. Marjorie was much more relaxed. If I were invited to a formal dinner and arrived with mismatched socks of differing colors, she wouldn't care. She never made small things an issue. I think she always felt there was no use in worrying about those little things.

One year there was an Argentinian family whose infant required a liver transplant. They sought the expertise of American transplant medicine. Marjorie and Ed offered for them to stay at the house. They really shared their home with everyone. And there was such diversity that everybody learned something from each other. There are so many differences that divide people but living together under one roof demonstrates that we are more alike than different.

I've always wondered, "What's the definition of a family?" For me, I think it's a group of people from different backgrounds coming together and choosing to stay together because it inspires each of us to be the best version of ourselves.

The one who started it all and kept us together through the years was my American mom, Marjorie Margolies.

CHAPTER 2

How It All Began

*The future belongs to those who believe in the
beauty of their dreams.*

– ELEANOR ROOSEVELT

THE 1960S WAS A DECADE drenched in extremes. Our society was in the midst of a cultural shift, birthed from the wholesome uniformity of the 1950s where "traditional" nuclear families were depicted as not only ideal but compulsory. From newspaper ads to television shows, the ingredients for a happy family life were unwavering and soberingly clear: a father as head of the house with a respectable job outside the home and a dutiful mother who derived pleasure from the three Cs—cooking, cleaning, and childbearing. When it came to children, the expectation was a boy first and then a girl, with natural birth as the only possible method: the ideal nuclear family formed in the ideal way. I knew that scenario well. I'd grown up in the previous two decades in such an environment.

As a dutiful Jewish American couple, Herbert and Mildred Margolies, my parents, followed the formula closely. We were nestled comfortably in the newly dawning societal construct of middle-class suburbia outside of Baltimore and then Philadelphia. My sister Phylis came along first. Because of my sister's health issues, Mom devoted herself to caring for Phylis. I made my debut three years later. Father/breadwinner, check; mother/homemaker, check; and two children, check. There wasn't a son in sight, but it was close enough that we fit the mold.

In the mid-1960s, I was a single working woman in my early twenties. The Civil Rights movement was in full swing, and women's liberation bubbled just beneath the surface, a dormant geyser ready to erupt. It was a time when many young people felt disenfranchised and disillusioned with the ideals foisted on them by the previous generation. We were determined to effect change...or try to.

I graduated from college and had ideas about things that I wanted to do, such as travel the world. How could I fit my youthful ambitions into the rigid mold of the status quo? I decided to put traveling for a living on hold and teach. I set that goal, got a degree, and soon I was living my dream, or what I thought was my dream. I taught Spanish and Social Studies for two years and was unceremoniously fired because I reported the kid of an important person for cutting my class. It was clear that I had a lot to learn about navigating not only the working world but the internal machinations that come along with it.

My mother tried to console me the best she knew how. "They only fired you because of your strong principles."

"That's one way to look at it, Mom."

Regardless of the reason, no one likes feeling unwanted, and getting canned is the ultimate kiss-off. Ever the overachiever, I was already having my midlife crisis...in my early twenties. That sting temporarily deflated my professional ambition like a day-old party balloon. I'd bought into the professional façade of teaching for a few years, then maybe taking on more responsibility, possibly moving into education administration ten or fifteen years down the road. I saw myself as the relatable teacher, the one who students could confide in because I was young and in touch with the changing times, a "today woman"... until my conscience got the better of me. So that's what doing the right thing gets you in this world. Mom was right. I was just too damned principled for my own good. Hell, at least I knew I'd never be a politician.

Ever the optimist, I tried my best to view the situation in a positive light, a vocational signpost if you will. *Veer left at the fork in your career path. Great job lies just ahead.* I was smarter now, more worldly, a wisdom born from pain. It was time to take stock, reassess. Being fired had sent a clear signal that while I loved working with children, teaching probably wasn't the vocation for me. I'm sure I could have found another position and re-engaged with the academic world; this time savvier about interpersonal relationships; but I decided I should shift my focus to something else that I loved besides children.

First, I needed to prioritize. I was good at making lists, in fact I loved the entire process: brainstorming, arranging, organizing, and the ultimate reward, ticking off the accomplishments. I found it quite satisfying. It felt like I was a student again. Plus, we were in a new era of emerging female empowerment. The world was finally allowing us to make our own mark, without a man by our side if we chose to do so. Professional options for women were slowly expanding, and I was eager, ambitious, and filled with that youthful idealism that reality gradually chips away at with each disappointment and setback.

I had a background in athletics. I'd led cycle tours in college, and part of my responsibility had been to guide teenagers on bicycles all over the U.S. One year we even traveled to Mexico and the next year to Israel and the Middle East, seeing the sights, soaking in the culture, and crashing at youth hostels along the way.

So, after my teaching misstep, I parlayed that experience into a job as head of the neighborhood youth corps in Philadelphia. During that time, I also volunteered at WUHY-FM, a small educational radio station.

Back to my list: what was it that I enjoyed doing? Being around children, of course, but what else? I'd always enjoyed writing. Term papers and research projects were a personal favorite and a skill on which I prided myself. Writing assignments energized me because I knew how to select an engaging topic, perform the necessary research, and tell a comprehensive, compelling, and entertaining story. When such an assignment was announced, the wheels started turning and ideas tumbled around in my brain while my classmates moaned and shifted in their seats.

Ok, so what else did I enjoy? Traveling was a big one. I'd spent my formative years in the perfectly respectable outskirts of Baltimore and Philadelphia, but I wanted to see more, much more. I found visiting new places fascinating, from the architecture to the societal differences. Certainly, the United States offered limitless opportunities to experience each and every state and territory for a complete immersion in the diversity within the borders of our own country. When I thought of international travel, my mind raced as I wondered what it would be like to visit such incredible cultures that had evolved throughout the centuries.

The last item on my list was "people." I loved children, but my curiosity went much further. I found people simply fascinating, from their thoughts and mannerisms to their motivations and inner passions. I enjoyed learning why people lived the way they do and made the choices they made. Why were we so similar yet so different all over the world? We all have unique stories and experiences to share, but we also have so much in common.

With that final piece of the puzzle, my list basically boiled down to three things: writing, traveling, and connecting with people. I just had to find a job that included those ingredients, and it would surely be where I'd find satisfaction and fulfillment.

While I was volunteering at the Philadelphia radio station, I knew that I had a lot to learn to determine if it was the right career path for me. It was part of the Eastern Educational Radio Network, a precursor to today's NPR, and I was given my own news program called *Filadelphia Folio*. It was quite exciting, and I was eager to absorb as much knowledge as possible. It was a challenge to learn how to modulate my voice, control my speech patterns, and use verbal inflection to punctuate the scripts that I wrote for each program.

I spent the day preparing for the show, and for a half hour each night, my voice was transmitted to radios throughout the city. In reality, that tiny radio station had an embarrassingly modest reach. It was like a college station without the captive audience. To make sure I had at least another dedicated listener, my mother took her eyebrow pencil and marked the exact location on my grandmother's radio dial so she could find the station easily.

It was so homegrown that I often felt like my parents and grandmother were the only ones tuning in, and on some days they may have been. One evening on the drive home, I put the window down just a crack and felt the night air blow my hair. It smelled of the city, a potpourri of pollen, exhaust fumes, and asphalt, with a hint of something burning in the distance. I realized in that moment that, for once, my life felt like it was going in the right direction.

While I loved teaching, I'd never had that feeling of accomplishment and gratification. It felt good to do something that I found challenging and enjoyable. Despite the fact that I was only a volunteer, a light bulb went off. I had a realization that the stars were aligning for me, the pieces were falling into place, my own ah-ha moment. I was a single woman finding her way in a man's world.

After a year at WUHY/WHYY radio station, I was ready for more challenges, more experiences, just...more. One morning, I downed a strong cup of coffee, dressed in the most professional outfit I had, and drove to WCAU-TV, Philadelphia's CBS owned and operated station. I walked into the office of a man named Barry Nemcoff, and in my best radio voice confidently asked him for a job as a television reporter.

"Why would I hire you?" he asked pointedly.

I took his question as a challenge. "I have a background in political science, languages, and sports, and that could be advantageous to you."

"To be honest, you may be a bit overqualified for this position in terms of education," he said.

I took a breath. "I enjoy my work at the radio station, and I'm confident that I can master the journalism aspect of the job. What I find exciting is exploring the human-interest angle of every story. I'm confident that with your guidance, I can do it."

I drove home without a job, but I didn't feel the defeat that I'd felt when I was fired. In fact, it was quite the opposite. Perhaps I was delusional, but when he said, "If we get an opening, I'll call you," I took that as a "yes." He could have easily said he wasn't interested but he hadn't said that at all. After conducting many radio interviews, I'd become fairly adept at reading people and evaluating their credibility.

There was a commentator on Washington's Channel 10 TV news program named Donald Barnhouse. He provided thoughtful commentary for that station and was something of a local celebrity. We became close friends, and I confided in him that I had approached Barry at WCAU about a job. He was a great sounding board since he had been in the industry much longer than I and always gave me great advice. He also told me that he'd tuned in to my radio show so that made almost half a dozen verified listeners!

In April of 1968, about eight months after my TV station ambush, Barry called with a job offer. He explained that it was only a summer internship, but that was fine by me. He asked when I could start. I said, "Give me a couple of weeks and I'll be ready for work!" I later found out that my friend Donald had put in a good word for me, and for that I've been eternally grateful.

Each day at the TV station was a learning experience. To begin with, I was the only white female working there. The only other woman was African American, and the rest were men, and most of them white. If a nicely dressed woman walked in, one of my coworkers would whisper, "she must be after your job!" They couldn't fathom the possibility of more women working there. Maybe she was after *their* jobs!

(Today, I'm so grateful for the changes that have taken place in workplaces across the country. When Joe Biden gave his first presidential address with women standing behind him on either side of the podium, it struck me how far we have come in just a few decades.)

Every day at the news station, I was bombarded with an avalanche of new information, new experiences, new challenges. I learned so much about not only the industry but myself as well. I not only had to navigate the interpersonal workings of the news station but also the intricacies of being on camera and presenting an image that was trustworthy, appealing, and watchable. With Barry as my boss and mentor, I was able to absorb his years of knowledge and then apply them in a way that worked for me. As an eager beginner, I put all my energy into the challenge, and it seemed to pay off. I was offered a full-time position at the end of the summer. My TV news career had officially begun.

The stories I brought to our audience were as varied and nuanced as I'd hoped they would be, but being a single woman in a predominantly male industry was no easy feat. I faced many roadblocks because of my gender and the workplace culture, but eventually I learned to use it to my advantage. Many people that I talked to while working on a story found me approachable and easy to confide in, so much so that I became known around the station as the reporter who could get the interview that had eluded others. My niche became human interest stories, those where hardworking citizens of Philadelphia and the surrounding area had experiences to share, experiences that other people found intriguing and relatable.

At one point, I successfully pitched to Barry a series of stories on adoption with the focus on Korean children who were labeled as "hard to place." I became friendly with many families in the area who had adopted children from Korea by attending picnics that were sponsored by Holt International, a U.S. adoption agency that pioneered international adoptions with a focus on Korean children. Their goal was to bring families and adopted children together to meet and make friends with other kids just like them. Many of the children were infants, and others were considered "challenging" for various reasons.

While I was covering those picnics, I began thinking about the idea of adopting a child myself. Even though I was a single woman, I could provide a stable home for a child in need, especially an older or hard-to-place child. As part of my research, I went to the agencies in Philadelphia, and said, "I'd be interested in adopting as a single parent." However, most of the kids available at that time were African American, and the priority was to place them with parents of the same race, if possible, and I certainly understood why that was important.

My life had been built on one challenge after another, and I'm sure both of my parents found my unflagging persistence noble but somewhat frustrating. Their generation focused on achieving stability and conformity, of reducing the element of surprise, of reveling in peaceful predictability. They saw me as the daughter who was guaranteed to bend the rules, push the boundaries.

That indomitable spirit, that yearning to do "more," may have evolved from my participation in sports early on, thriving on competition, setting goals and surpassing them. While being an elite athlete culminated in an invitation to try out for the 1958 U.S. Olympic team in track and field and becoming the southeast Atlantic women's broad jumping champion, that discipline and dedication never left me.

What my mother called "an independent streak" was the only way I knew how to live. My plan had always been to explore opportunities, ask questions, and rarely take "no" for an answer. That self-motivation served me well as an investigative reporter hustling to find a compelling story better than the last, constantly creating content to feed the insatiable appetite of the viewing audience.

My need to challenge convention was something my parents never fully understood and that was crystal clear when I began to talk about my interest in adoption...for myself. They were concerned about my future, knowing how hard I'd worked to get my career started. I was breaking the mold of what was expected from a young single woman, and I enjoyed surprising people, showing that I could fulfill my dreams regardless of societal norms.

Still, I found myself wondering if I was ready to take on the responsibility of a hard-to-place child. My mother had given up her dream of a career in graphic design to fulfill her wifely and motherly duties. She never complained, but she was an accomplished fine artist, so I knew what she had sacrificed.

I anticipated that my mother would be upset when I shared

my thoughts on adoption with her. To be fair, she'd seen me struggle until I found my career, and now, in her eyes, I was going to mess that up by adopting.

"If you need a child so badly, why don't you just have your own?" she'd suggested once I broke the news.

It was certainly a possibility, but the decision didn't feel right. I wasn't ready to bring a child into this world. I'd rather help one who was already here. At least that was my thought process. I also had to remind her that I was raised by parents who themselves had sponsored two girls to the U.S. at my urging: one from Spain, the other from Bolivia.

I try to keep in touch with them to this day. Vicky Arechaga now lives in Oregon. She has three grown children and five grandchildren. We talk frequently, and she sent me this letter about her time with the family.

> Marjorie and I met in Bilbao, Spain, when she came as part of an American group of college students with the Experiment in International Living. Our bond was immediate, we became friends and sisters forever.
>
> When my husband and I decided to move to the US, we were stunned by the amount of paperwork involved and the unpleasant surprise that we would need a sponsor to vouch for us, even though I had been born in the US and carried an American passport. Of the 200 million people living in the States, I knew ONE! I contacted Marjorie and she assured me that her father would take care of it. This man, this family, did not know us at all, nevertheless they sponsored a very young, naïve, and pregnant couple, welcomed us into their home and became our forever family!
>
> Mildred was a vision of sophistication in a beautiful caftan and Herb was a tall serious man, with a twinkle in his eyes and a wicked sense of humor. In that instant our lives

changed; we didn't know the language, we didn't know the customs, but we had support, we had a family!! They were Nanny and Pop-pop to my children; they were role models for us.

Mildred was a wonderful artist; her paintings filled their apartment and ours, but none were as beautiful to me as the quick sketch that she made of my newborn son, whom I was told was having trouble breathing and was put on a ventilator. Having just had a C-section, I was unable to go to the nursery to see him. Mildred grabbed the first piece of paper that she saw, a barf bag on the night table, rushed to the nursery and came back a few minutes later with a sketch of a peaceful baby. This drawing, to this day, means more to me than a canvas portrait in any museum!

They were with me at the birth of each of my three children. I remember the stern nuns at Lady of Lourdes Hospital shooing Herb out of my room because he was making me laugh so hard that I was also crying in pain from the incision.

When my daughter had her First Communion, the entire pew was filled with this wonderful Jewish family who followed the rituals of standing, kneeling, and bowing their heads as if they had been raised Catholic, discreetly watching what everybody else was doing. When each child went up to the altar to receive communion, with parents and grandparents, Mildred whispered to me that she would go, too, because she didn't want to embarrass my daughter not having any grandparents behind her. Of course, I assured her that it was not necessary, but it stayed in my heart and I'm sure the Lord had a chuckle and was very pleased.

Whenever they were visiting, Herb insisted on going to the supermarket with us. At the register he would always play this game, toss a coin and whoever calls it pays for the groceries. Of course, he was cheating, but we were never able to catch him, and of course he always paid! His dry humor was legendary, and his kindness and patience knew no bounds. Mildred taught me how to cook, how to set a proper table, and to accept everybody, no matter how different we may be.

No matter how independent I saw myself as a single woman in the revolutionary 1960s, I was now wondering what it would be like to have a child. Was I ready for that responsibility? To be brutally honest, was I ready to focus on someone other than myself? Fulfilling my own professional dreams was a form of self-care that I wasn't sure I could relinquish. Then I realized that just because that's what women were encouraged to do—stay home, care for a house and children, shelve any professional goals—I didn't have to do that. I could break that mold, too. After all, it was almost 1970, and young people were changing the world.

I knew my decision was as important, if not more so, than deciding to marry. After months of soul searching and talking with others, I decided to move forward with investigating the idea of adoption as a single woman.

It was crucial for me to consider how the child would fit into my routine, into my hectic work schedule, into my social life, and into the lives of my parents to whom I was awfully close. I was realistic. I couldn't adopt a child who had special needs. That ruled out a wide swath of hard-to-place children: the physically handicapped and those who needed constant care. They needed someone at home to dedicate their full attention. But I could take a child who was "too old" or who hadn't been adopted for any number of reasons.

When I started exploring my options by making calls to local agencies, I already knew most people interested in adoption wanted babies, preferably newborns. But there were so many children—older ones—who desperately needed loving homes. However, there were all kinds of rules that barred me from moving forward.

A form letter I received in 1969 from an association in China did not give me great hope.

> *Dear Mr. & Mrs.*
>
> *We understand that you wish to adopt a baby from our nursery. We are enclosing herewith a copy each of Stipulations for Application, Application for Adoption, Individual Adoptive Family Survey Form, and Declaration of Intent.*
>
> *We also need the following documents:*
>
> *1. Certificate of marriage.*
>
> *2. Certificate of health for both husband and wife.*
>
> *3. Certificate issued by a public hospital certifying the wife's inability to conceive if she is under 38 years of age.*
>
> *4. Certificate of occupation – a letter from the organization you work for is sufficient.*
>
> *5. Financial Statement:*
>
> *a. Letter from you concerning your bank account, savings, and credit extended.*
>
> *b. Certificate of ownership of house or property – if any.*
>
> *c. Certificate of any other source of income – if any.*
>
> *We would appreciate it if you would fill out these forms and sent to this association at your earliest convenience.*
>
> *In response to the actual demand, we have been obliged to impose on anyone who adopts a child from our nursery the following charges:*
>
> *1. US $300 for child living expenses prior to the date on which the child is chosen for adoption, equipment, nursing tendance, subsidy for social worker's home visits, birth registration, notary, transportation, etc.*

2. US $100 for going through procedures of sending a child to a foreign country, such as: household certificate, photo, copies of documents, physical examination, exit permit, passport, visa, local transportation, subsidy for social worker, etc.

3. US $50 monthly for the child's living expenses starting from the date on which the child is chosen for adoption and ending at the time when taken by the parents. During this period, medical fees will be charged to them if the child needs medical care.

The above-mentioned payments can be made after the approval of your adoption by our committee.

Should you have any further questions concerning these certificates, please do not hesitate to write.

All good wishes.

I continued to call other organizations, and the more I was denied, the more determined I became. I must have contacted a dozen adoption agencies. One of them had the following requirements:

All childless couples, foreign and native, who meet the following qualifications are eligible to apply for baby adoption, provided they furnish certificates of physical examination and birth inability.

1. Legally married.

2. Childless or having too few children.

3. Possessing a lodging place.

4. On a job earning sufficient salary to maintain a decent living.

5. Mentally and physically healthy.

6. 20 to 50 years older than the adopted child.

7. Willing to be investigated on family background, personality, financial status, and other related aspects from any possible sources.

8. With consent of his or her spouse.

9. Able to secure a guarantor who has a job.

10. Children under 14 years only are eligible to be adopted by couples living in the United States in conformance with the US Immigration Regulation.

Then I decided to try Holt International. Their headquarters was in Eugene, Oregon, and of course they remembered my news stories about the picnics they sponsored. They informed me that one of the first steps would be to have a home study completed as part of the adoption process.

So, I contacted a wonderfully understanding woman named Roberta Andrews from the Children's Aid Society of Pennsylvania, which acted as an adoption liaison agency. She agreed to complete the home study of me and my family. Once that had been done, the adoption process was in full swing, at least on my part.

In May of 1970, my parents were fortuitously planning a trip to Expo '70, the Tokyo World's Fair, and invited me along. The visit would be perfect because I could spend time in Tokyo and then hopefully visit the Holt Agency in Korea to not only finish up some reporting to complete my adoption news series but also investigate the possibility of finding a child. I wasn't given a crew, only a 16mm camera that I could use to shoot my own film. Still, I found the theme of the expo a sign of encouragement. It was, "progress and harmony for mankind."

As I detailed in my book *They Came to Stay*, published in 1976, I was able to meet with a man named Jack Thesis to discuss the adoption process, my journey thus far, and my hopes for a child, an older child, and preferably a girl. We talked about my job, my motives, and my goals for a family. He also had a copy of the home study that had already been completed. When asked the kind of child I was interested in, I hesitated. Then I finally came out with what I then thought was important. I wasn't sure what to say, so I responded that I wanted a child who was hard to place, alert, and flexible. Then I explained that I'd be working on a news story for a few days before I had to leave. Mr. Thesis promised to contact me before I left Korea.

Next, I went straight to work locating the people I needed to interview, visiting various locations throughout Korea, and shooting footage myself along the way. Professionally, it was satisfying to close the loop on the story, something reporters didn't often get to experience. We usually reported a story and were left to wonder how things turned out. Did the criminal get caught? Was the stolen property returned? Had those displaced by a fire found a new home? However, this time, I was able to get closure, and perhaps more.

I learned so much visiting the agency and hearing about the challenges they faced trying to place children in stable homes. At the time, it was estimated that approximately eight Korean children were displaced daily, for a variety of reasons. Despite the crowded conditions at the Holt Agency, it was gratifying to see how much attention the children received. Some needed individual love so badly that they wouldn't let go of my hand as we walked through the hallways together. Others wouldn't smile or respond to my open arms because they assumed I, like hundreds before me, would disappear when my visit was over, never to be heard from again.

At the Children's Hospital, a social worker showed me the "holding area" where many of the kids were placed when they first arrived. I was told 30 to 50 percent of the children died there, before ever reaching an orphanage. The hopeless looks on their faces, the heat, the smells, it all combined to create an atmosphere that was almost unbearable. Those waifs of all sizes, ages, and racial mixtures, many of whom reached out for my legs as I walked down the corridors, were forever etched into my mind.

One of the towns that was responsible for a large number of these helpless children sat snugly near an army camp. The Korean women who "serviced" the white soldiers were on one side of the street, those who serviced Blacks on the other. I saw a three-year-old mixed-race child taken from his prostitute mother as she wailed and cried in the street. Representatives from the orphanage had explained to her what she already knew: the little boy would be difficult to place and was considered adoptable only as long as he was tiny and babylike. By the time he became a gangly nine-year-old, he'd have lost his chance, and Korean society would not accept him either. Mixed races were outcasts, stared at, constantly abused.

With one day left in Korea, I had conflicting emotions. Professionally, I'd accomplished my mission and gathered plenty of material for my story. However, on a personal level, I'd held out hope that somehow, some way, I'd meet a potential adoptee despite the countless times I'd been told it would never happen for me as a single woman.

While I was at my hotel packing, I got a call and was elated to hear Jack's voice on the other end of the line. By some miracle, he said that due to the circumstances, they had been able to fast-track the process and locate a potential match for me, a seven-year-old girl named Lee Heh Kyung. He wanted me to come by in the morning. My flight was scheduled for 9:00 a.m., but I quickly told him I'd find a flight that left later in the day. She could be the one, I thought! I dialed my parents in Tokyo and shared the news. They offered to come with me, but I told them it wasn't necessary. This was something I would do on my own.

After a sleepless night, on June 5, 1970, at 9:30, I went to the Holt offices in Seoul and there she was...Lee Heh Kyung or Heh Kyung Lee (since in Korea the surname is always put first). Her name was phonetically pronounced "Lee Hay Kee-young." I took a moment to let the syllables tumble around in my mind.

The small girl stuck out an assured little hand and beamed "Haw doo yoo dooo?" (I later found out that this and "Tenk you berry mouch" were her only English expressions.) I could see she was happy, alert, and responsive, and I wondered what was clicking away in her little mind, but we had only a few precious hours together.

After giving me a few tidbits of information about her past, it was time for me to catch my rescheduled flight. To continue building our bond, they brought her to the airport to see me off so that we could spend as much time together as possible. As we waited for my plane, she ordered chocolate ice cream and shyly offered it to everyone. Her *bomo* (caretaker) kept on saying "she's number one" as she held up her finger. I said goodbye to her and went home with the biggest hurdle still before me, getting her into the United States. I already missed being with her, but I had her official orphanage photo to look at. Her hair was cropped squarely, and a card held in front of her read "Lee Heh Kyung, #7335."

I immediately went home to share the details with my parents. Knowing that my mind was made up, they were both excited by the possibility of an addition to the family. My father contacted an amazing lawyer, Isidor Ostroff, who had helped them with my two internally sponsored sisters many years prior. Now it was my turn. Through his knowledge of the intricacies and technicalities of the Immigration and Adoption laws, he was able to work out my soon-to-be daughter's admission with the State Department and the Immigration Service on a student visa. She would be the youngest student ever to enter the United States, but I had to wait for notification.

Much later, once everything was arranged, I received THE call from a woman at the Holt Agency. "I want to give you as much time as I can...your little girl will be coming. On Monday."

To say I was stunned would be a ridiculous understatement. I had had a two-and-a-half-year pre-adoptive pregnancy, and I was now delivering.

She would arrive in Chicago where, by coincidence, I had planned to go that weekend to visit relatives. Late Monday afternoon found my aunt, two cousins, and me awaiting the plane from Seoul. There we stood with two other families also waiting for Korean children, a television crew, and a bevy of onlookers, each of us lost in our own thoughts about what was going to happen over the next several hours. Shortly before 5:00, the plane arrived, and a sleepy child was carried off by a chaperone. I was told she had stayed up most of the 18-hour trip babbling away, and half an hour before the plane landed had dozed off, only to wake to a battery of television lights and a squadron of people fawning over her and chattering in a language she didn't understand.

My cousin Chuck remembers the day well:

When I was about 15 years old, my mother, Babette Henschel, announced that our cousin Marjorie was coming to town to visit. Marjorie was always one of my favorites! She was one of my mom's sister's daughters. She was 10 or 12 years older than I and very worldly (out of college and had an exciting job) and an all-around great person. There was much excitement because the reason she was coming to Chicago was to receive her new daughter Lee Heh who was arriving from Korea. I had heard talk amongst my parents of the attempts by Marjorie to adopt a child but hadn't really followed it too closely. But it was all done, and her first child was arriving at O'Hare the next day.

In 1970, as today, O'Hare International Airport was a major connecting airport with many international flights and quite busy. Unlike today, in 1970 you could just park your car and go to the gate to meet your arriving friends and relatives. We went out to O'Hare and I had no idea what to expect. We went to the gate to meet Marjorie's new daughter and as passengers came off the plane, there was this little Korean girl no more than 5 or 6 and no more than 30 or 35 pounds. A little shy and uncertain, but amazingly happy to see us! A group of veritable strangers and her new extended family.

To my recollection, she didn't speak or understand much English. Lee Heh seemed very willing to go with the flow and happy to have me just pick her up and carry her on my hip, and off we went to our house in the suburbs. The next few days was a blur of my sisters and me playing with Lee Heh in our living room on the carpet, eating food that Lee Heh had never tried before and trying to communicate with this beautiful little girl from halfway around the world. Before I realized it, she and Marjorie were gone to Philadelphia.

I don't know if it was the fact that I was there when she arrived in the United States or just a special connection, but to this day, Lee Heh and I have an enduring love and a special connection. We still refer to each other as our favorite cousin.

We stayed in the windy city that night. I probably got up 20 times to make sure she had not fallen from her bed since I knew she'd only slept on mats before. She played with "the cousins" as if she'd known them all her life and ate her first American lunch like a champ, the fork and the knife must have been terribly strange for her. She had the surreal experience of watching her own arrival on television as if it were the most natural thing in the world. I could have "Americanized" her name but decided to call her Lee Heh Margolies.

A week later, I enrolled her in the neighborhood grade school, two blocks from our Philadelphia apartment. During the first week, I would say *hakkio* (school) in Korean as we passed the school, and she would firmly shake her head "no." Finally, with the help of a Korean friend and a well-thumbed translation dictionary, I learned she was ashamed to go because she spoke no English.

I dropped her off on the first day of school with some hesitation because of the language barrier. The students in her class were standing in a line, and I watched as she marched right up to the front and measured her height against the first child. Since she was the littlest one there, she thought she should be in the front of the line. I was amazed at how confident and self-assured she seemed at her new school.

Several months later, her teacher, Mrs. DeSantis, walked the children out. The kids told me that the teacher had said to them that she was going to call on Lee Heh to read and that they should not laugh. "Understand that this is not her language," she'd said. The kids told me, "She's the best reader in the class." And they applauded.

I often wondered what had happened during the first few years of Lee Heh's life. No one knew for sure. I suspected that she had lived in South Korea before being taken to the orphanage because she had never seen snow. Maybe she had lived in a small village because when she'd see a Vietnamese village on television, she'd say "Look! Korea." I don't think she lived by the sea because she'd never seen a boat. It was like snapping together the puzzle pieces of her life.

At first Lee Heh seemed to have erased most of those memories, but little by little she talked about the past. One day when playing with two friends who were siblings, her feelings unexpectedly surfaced. The two were fighting, as any normal brother and sister will. Lee Heh pulled them aside separately and said to each that they shouldn't fight with one another, that she had had two brothers, and now she had none. To the girl, she said, "You are the oldest, and should take the responsibility of the big sister." To the boy she said, "You are the man."

Another time Lee Heh came home from school and told me a little girl had been stealing her morning snack. When the other children told her to tell the teacher, she said she wouldn't. "I thought maybe the little girl was sad." This from a child whose legs were slightly bent with rickets when I first met her because of improper diet, who, when she went to the orphanage for meals, had taken food in her mouth, birdlike, to feed other children who were hungrier. I cried softly that night.

People sometimes asked me how she reacted to the men I dated, and they to her. At first dating was difficult because naturally she saw the men in my life as a threat to our bond together. But after constant reassurance, she became more certain of the permanency and stability of our relationship and accepted other people in it, so sure and so accepting that she once said to a friend of mine, "Will you marry us?" That was slightly awkward.

I, on the other hand, made it very clear that Lee Heh and I came as a team, that I couldn't consider seriously dating a man who did not support my life choices. Being a parent was my new reality, and I approached it with my usual resolve. Much to their credit, my parents were invaluable as they assisted me along the way. Since we lived close to each other, they stepped in to help when I had to work. They loved having an instant grandchild right around the corner, and it showed in their devotion to little Lee Heh.

In fact, when she was first put into daycare after school, the teacher was the one to escort the children from the school to the daycare. My father would show up at that time just to make sure Lee Heh arrived safely at daycare. Then he would even pick her up if I wasn't able to.

Adopting Lee Heh was an amazing experience, way beyond what I'd imagined. I learned so much and even surprised myself with how I could balance my work responsibilities with motherhood. Having help from my family made all things possible, and I was grateful for how we had managed to weave together a strong, loving, harmonious family.

During my adventures in adoption and building a family, I had to juggle the challenges of a demanding career and its impact on the various stages of my home life. It's something almost all women have learned to navigate over the years, but when I started out, it was not as common for a single mother to be so passionate about her career path and her family. She was expected to focus primarily on her children, and maybe take on a job, if necessary, but certainly not a career. My intention was always to do both, even as a single mother. I never even considered that I'd have to choose one over the other. To be fulfilled, I wanted a satisfying career *and* a family.

At one point in my career, I won a CBS news fellowship at Columbia. To the surprise of many, I took a year off from my job to hone my journalism skills. Then I returned to WCAU. Soon, I was offered a job in New York as part of an investigative team for the 6:00 news called *News 4 New York*. Fortunately, my parents were able to watch Lee Heh at their home in Philadelphia, just a short train ride away. Then, I finally found a homey one-bedroom New York apartment in a good location for work. It faced the East River, there was a playground nearby, and I could afford it.

My parents helped with the transition, staying with me and Lee Heh while we got the apartment furnished and decorated. I had two twin beds in the bedroom for me and Lee Heh, and a pullout sofa in the living room for my parents. They helped ease us into a routine by getting Lee Heh set up at the United Nations International School where she would go that fall, while I was trying to establish myself in my new job. It was a struggle that most parents know well.

While Lee Heh was off at a sleepaway camp that summer, I was asked to do a story about my adoption journey for our news program. She and I had done some interviews in the past because of the publicity that surrounded the first international adoption by a single person, but I wanted to get away from that. I didn't want her to think that was "normal." Yet, I finally agreed to do the story.

This is the script of that story complete with ellipses to show my pauses while reading on the news.

There's a cardinal rule in journalism (actually in most fields)... it says you never begin by telling how difficult your story is. Well, I'm going to break that rule by telling you how hard it is for me to do this story.

It's about my little girl, Lee Heh Margolies, and the only thing I can assure you from the outset is...this is not an objective study. This report comes from a very prejudiced, very doting mother who happens in this case to be, only by chance, a reporter.

Over four years ago, I did a series on "hard-to-place children" (children who have little chance of being adopted)... and I got carried away. The little girl I adopted is Korean... I'm single...and United States law doesn't permit someone to bring a child into the country for adoption purposes without a spouse. So, I'll start from the top....

I went to Korea to follow up my story. Korea has a tremendous child desertion problem (about eight children are left each day). When I arrived at the orphanage...this is Holt Orphanage at Il San)...I told those in charge...I'd gladly adopt one of their children...and proceeded to do my story.

With camera and pen in hand, I learned the heartbreaking tales of hundreds of deserted children. Half die before they can be placed...many cannot be placed because of age, illness, or racial mixture. As I was getting ready to leave, the director of the orphanage came to me and said, "We've picked a child for you."

I met Lee Heh Kyung, who was considered too old to be placed, bright and early...June 5th, 1970...it was hard for me to believe that there was a good chance that this little girl would be with me for the rest of my life.

Four months later...with the help of a perfectly marvelous lawyer...Lee Heh arrived in Chicago...she entered the United States as an alien on a student visa. She was bewildered, didn't speak a word of English...but somehow knew things would be bright.

What you'll see next are Pop-Pop pictures...those awful home movies of loving grandparents...and I burden you with them because I think they are just darling...and they give you a chance to see what an easy adjustment Lee Heh has made.

Last November, Lee Heh and I moved to New York... during the past year she attended the United Nations International School. Each morning, I walked her to school and then come into work...but I'll let Lee Heh tell you the rest....

I interviewed the subject in the living room of her apartment...she was given a dummy microphone...I interviewed her and asked, "What does adoption mean?"...she replied, "No one can take you way."... she won.

On the day I adopted Lee Heh, I gave her a picture...of the two of us...in it was a heart...with a poem on it...which I'd like to leave you with...it goes....

> *Not flesh of my flesh,*
> *Nor bone of my bone,*
> *But still miraculously my own,*
> *Never forget,*
> *Not even for a minute,*
> *You weren't born under my heart,*
> *But in it.*

The story evoked a positive response from the audience, and Lee Heh was absolutely amazing on camera. I was surprised to find out how natural and engaging she was. In the other interviews, I was constantly being told how wonderful she'd been and how the audience responded so well to her. We did several national shows and she never failed to charm them. On *The Dick Cavett Show*, Dick, the host, knew that she'd been declared the best reader in her first-grade class, so he asked her to read the commercial intro on the teleprompter.

She looked at the camera and sounded it out. "Banker's Life Insurance of Dez Moinzes." She had done it with such ease and innocence that it was TV gold. Dick continued to use that phrase for many years afterwards, often adding "as a friend of mine says...Dez Moinzes."

He also asked who her favorite person on TV was, likely angling for a compliment, but she didn't know him since his show was on later at night. Lee Heh said without hesitation, "Marlo Thomas" who was then in a sitcom called *That Girl*. (I was often told that I resembled Marlo so that may have been another reason for Lee Heh's answer.) Later, Marlo's friend contacted me, and all of us met in person. It was wonderful.

Once Lee Heh and I settled into our New York life, things were easier than I'd anticipated. I had some unusual hours, but I was able to make it work for the two of us. We continued getting requests for more interviews which put me in the position of being an on-camera reporter being interviewed for a story about my own life. It was a bit surreal.

Four years after that adoption, I got the idea to try again, maybe a sister for Lee Heh, a child close in age. After a couple of years, I was able to adopt another girl, this time from Vietnam; however, the transition was not Lee Heh-esque.

CHAPTER 3

Answering Her Calls

At work, you think of the children you've left at home. At home,
you think of the work you've left unfinished. Such a struggle.

– CHARLOTTE PERKINS GILMAN, AMERICAN WRITER

IN 1973, AFTER A FEW YEARS of relative ease with Lee Heh, I was
still in awe of how effortless it had been. When I started the
adoption process, I'd been cautioned of the challenges I would
face, how going from a single career woman to an instant mother
would likely be a rude awakening. As with any first-time parent,
my entire life would experience an upheaval.

All of that was true. My situation was especially intense
because unlike a "bio-birth," I had little time for preparation.
Only a few hours after I got the call, I was immediately responsible for a seven-year-old girl, but that was fine with me. I
was ready, and we had a relatively easy four years together. So,
I was ready to do it again.

My mother always said I tried to do too much, and she never
understood my high energy level. So, she was not surprised when
I talked about possibly adopting again. My parents loved their

relationship with Lee Heh and their other grandchildren, so I think because that process had been so enjoyable, they were up for the challenge.

I had talked my news director into following up on some of the stories that I had done on adoption. So, I traveled to Vietnam in February of 1973 and stayed in downtown Saigon. I was able to visit several orphanages and learn about the culture.

Coincidentally, while I was there, I ran into the people from Holt who'd helped with Lee Heh's adoption. They were establishing a presence in Vietnam similar to their office in Korea. I told them that I was working on a news series and that I was considering adopting another child. They immediately asked if they could help since the first adoption had gone so well. The need was more dire than I'd initially realized when I found out that there were stories of mistreatment and even some children being restrained to manage their behavioral issues.

In Vietnam, they used orphanages as places that not only took in children without parents, but also housed and fed children temporarily for parents who couldn't care for them, usually due to financial difficulty. If possible, the parents would even visit their children on occasion with the hopes of taking them back home once their situation improved. Before the children could be adopted, if they had no parents, their closest relative had to give permission.

Due to the Vietnam War that raged on, many of the children were the product of a Vietnamese mother and an American serviceman. Sometimes called "Amerasians," they were stark reminders of an unpopular war and often faced discrimination from Vietnamese society as "children of the dust." These children would make national news in 1975 when President Gerald Ford ordered the evacuation of Vietnamese orphans through Operation Baby Lift. I covered the story that ended tragically when the first flight crashed, killing 138 people including 78 children. However, subsequent efforts were successful and over 3,000 children were evacuated to the United States.

I received a call that they had potentially found a child who they thought was half Vietnamese and half American. The photo they sent was of a little girl with short, dark curly hair and missing front teeth. There was a card held in front of her that read: Ho Thi Thu Nga VN/CF 12VN#64.30.1967. The first word was the family name, the second indicated a female, the next two words were her first name—Thu Nga. The abbreviations stood for "Vietnamese/Child Female" number 64, born on December 30, 1967.

Until that moment, Lee Heh had shown nothing but excitement when we talked about her having a sister. After looking at the photo, she said the girl looked more like me and people would think she was my biological daughter. I had expected a bit of apprehension on her part, so I wasn't surprised when it came up. I quickly reassured her that she would always be my daughter and that would never change.

After that, I talked with the Holt staff constantly to get updates on when the adoption could happen. The country was still in chaos, and an old problem returned. They did not legally allow single parents to adopt Vietnamese children. I needed an I-600 visa to get her in the United States and they were only given to married couples.

Jack Adams at Holt International was in Saigon and agreed to see what he could do to help the situation. Meanwhile, I consulted with Izzy once again about a student visa, but he wasn't confident that it would work in this situation. I was running into dead ends and wasn't ready to accept that. There had to be a way.

Jack said that the only option was to get a "parole" visa issued and sent to Saigon. It was a section of U.S. immigration law that allowed refugees to come to the states for "humanitarian" reasons. I reached out to some friends, with Izzy's help, and finally found a Congress member who was willing to make the request through Immigration and Naturalization Services. If I could get it issued, I was to send it via cable to Jack to see if he could bring the girl back on his upcoming return to the U.S.

Ultimately, I was disappointed that Jack had to return emptyhanded. Then I discovered that a "private bill" would have to go before Congress to allow the young girl to enter under special circumstances. Finally, Joshua Eilberg, a representative from Pennsylvania, was able to help.

IN THE HOUSE OF REPRESENTATIVES
January 23, 1974

Mr. Eilberg introduced the following bill; which was
referred to the committee on the Judiciary
A BILL
For the relief of Ho Thi Thu Nga.

Be it enacted by the Senate and House of Representatives
of the United States of American in Congress assembled,
That, in the administration of the Immigration and Nationality Act
Ho Thi Thu Nga may be classified as a child within the meaning
of section 101(b)(1)(F) of the Act,

And a petition filed in her behalf by Miss Marjorie Margolies,
A citizen of the United States may be approved pursuant to section 204
of the Act: Provided, That the natural parents or brothers or sisters of
the beneficiary shall not, by virtue of such relationship, be accorded any
right, privilege, or status under the Immigration and Nationality Act.

The bill went through successfully, and a month later I received a call that the little girl was on her way to the U.S.

Jack informed me that a woman had initially brought the child to Holt. She had told a story that the baby girl had been found in a garbage can outside a US Army base at around 15 days old, the umbilical cord still attached. The woman said she tried to take care of the child but couldn't do it. (We later learned the real story, that the woman was actually her mother and likely a prostitute.) Knowing the poor girl had experienced more than her share of challenges at such a young age, I wasn't sure what to expect. However, I had no idea just how much of an adjustment it would be.

In the meantime, Lee Heh and I discussed names that would best suit this new addition to the family since people frequently mispronounced Lee Heh's name. We wanted to avoid that issue and put a lot of thought into it. The child's name was Ho Thi Thu Nga, and we didn't think "Ho" was quite right for obvious reasons. As we looked through a book, Lee Heh saw one and said, "We should call her Holly."

When "Holly" arrived, we were quite excited, but it was as if we'd received a letter bomb that was just on the verge of detonation. She was accompanied by Nancy Bennett, the wife of the ambassador. I had met Nancy when I was in Vietnam, and she had agreed to chaperone Holly.

What I didn't know about my little bundle of chaos was that she was riddled with worms and parasites that would later infiltrate our home. It wasn't just the medical issues. Holly was frustrated with everything from the beginning. She seemed angry that she had been taken away from her homeland, and she talked nonstop in Vietnamese. It was tough to figure out what she was saying, but Nancy did her best to help since she spoke a bit of the language. We did what we could.

Nancy figured maybe she would just lie down and place Holly on top of her to stroke her back and soothe her. At one point she thought she had succeeded in calming the child but instead felt warm liquid traveling down her body as Holly peed all over her. (Despite that initiation, Nancy was fond of Holly and would check in often to see how she was doing.)

There was no getting around the fact that Holly was going to be a completely different adoption experience. She was incredibly stubborn and prone to tantrums. For example, we could be walking down the street, and if she saw something that caught her eye, like pictures of food on a restaurant window, and I told her no, she would lie down at the entrance of the eatery and refuse to move. I could either wait her out (which could possibly take hours) or physically pick her up to keep moving. Or when we went to get her new shoes, she would turn the shoe over and put her foot on the bottom to measure it because that's what they did in Vietnam, and then she would not let us put the shoes on to make sure they fit. As I quickly learned, everything was a struggle with her. Everything.

One of my fears came true when Lee Heh began to lose patience with her new sister. Holly's disruptions were the antithesis of Lee Heh's orderly mannerisms. Fortunately, because Lee Heh was so conscientious and such a pleaser, she gave it her best effort, but I could just see the writing on the wall.

For example, we thought it would be fun for all three of us to visit the circus. Holly was just starting to speak English. When I explained what the circus was, she kept saying, "I know animals! I don't want go circus." In order to leave the apartment, I had to pick her up so that we would make it on time. I flashed a weak smile at the doorman as she continued to flail her arms and legs. Once we got to the circus, Holly absolutely loved it. I should have been happy when she finally came around, but then it was almost impossible to get her to leave. What made matters worse was that I knew the struggle wouldn't be a learning experience for her. It would happen again and again with alarming regularity.

With most children, once they realize that their fears and objections are meritless, they begin to acquiesce. But not our Holly. Each tantrum only seemed to fuel the next. There was no sense of realization or understanding that cooperation would be better for everyone. No matter what the suggestion, her mind immediately went to "no," and she had to be convinced otherwise. In fact, my extraordinarily patient father, Pop-pop, even said to me, "Maybe we should send her back."

The beginning was extraordinarily challenging and then slowly but surely, she started to realize that we were going to love her. We weren't going to leave her. There wasn't anything she could do to make us give her up, but it was incredibly challenging.

A glimmer of hope flickered through early on when I found out how well she got along with others. She was a typical child in that way: challenging at home but much better behaved elsewhere. She loved camp and usually had no trouble making friends. She was a super athlete and really excelled when she was accepted into Hunter College Elementary School.

As a follow up to the story I did on Lee Heh's Korean adoption, I also did a story on adoptions in Vietnam.

> *Over 85% of all children in Vietnamese orphanages have not been released for adoption...The concept of the orphanage is a relatively new one here...before, if parents died...the family unit took care of the child. But the war has made that impossible for many poor families...in some cases the war has totally destroyed the family unit.*
>
> *Lee is five years old...an enchanting child who's been in this orphanage for four years...she is not free for adoption.*

Her father visits her once a year...and the nun wasn't sure if he had made it this year. Hanh is six, her uncle left her in this orphanage a year and a half ago...he hasn't been back to see her since. She has no parents. These children are the rule... not the exception.

By and large...the Vietnamese reject adoption as an alternative. First of all, there is a strong feeling among them that they've already lost several generations to a series of wars... bodies, even if they are orphaned bodies, must stay in the country. The Vietnamese also feel that the children should be brought up in their homeland...and that in many cases it was the Americans who put a lot of these children into orphanages to begin with...why now should they take them away? A majority of orphanages are either Catholic or Buddhist... most of the Catholic ones will not release their children to non-Catholics...and the Buddhist orphanages will not release their children at all. I was struck by the number of biracial children in one of the orphanages.

Vietnamese adoption law is based on an archaic French law which requires a parent to be 20 years older than the child, married and childless for 10 years...never having adopted before. That eliminates 90% of perspective adoptive parents. Until now, those requirements could be waived...but only by the signature of President Theiu. For the past two years, the American Embassy here has been inundated with requests for adoption...after several years of negotiations... things are finally opening up.

For the past two years, the Holt Children's Services Agency has been negotiating with the Vietnamese government to set up an adoption center here in Vietnam. Within the past two weeks, a contract has been signed...officials say it was all a matter of timing.

This is their new $80,000 facility which can house 100 children. They hope to begin full operation within the next several months.

Holt already has a long waiting list. Before it came, the only other recognized group was International Social Services. There are several "unofficial groups" which have managed to get children out of the country...purely on the up and up... but they could be closed down with ease.

What struck me about the children is their air of maturity...many are seasoned, cynical, and cunning. And they don't want to be. Get beneath that grown up veneer and you find a kid who wants to be held, tickled, stroked...loved.

Before I went to Vietnam, I read an article which talked of children caressing adults on the street...while one hugged... the other stripped the victim of everything and anything that wasn't anatomically attached...I don't mean to sound like an instant expert...I'm sure that goes on...but it's the exception not the rule...and it's done for survival not sport.

When I got a call from work to do the early morning "cut-ins" as part of the *Today Show*, I was torn. I wanted to do it and it was a good move for my career, but I had to figure out what to do with the girls. They were 10 and 6 at the time, and this would require me to leave at 5:00 in the morning.

I called a friend from work, Jeanne Lee, who was willing to help. She stayed over the night before so that I could sneak out early without disturbing the children. I encouraged her to let the girls watch the news in the morning so they could see that I was working, especially Holly who couldn't speak English yet.

Once the show was over, I immediately called them to hear Holly squeaking into the phone, "Mommy! Mommy on TV!" I did the next segment and then hurried home. It was one of those mommy moments where you just have to make it work.

Having Lee Heh, a relatively adaptable child, as my first helped me get my sea legs, and I needed those and more for my precocious Holly. Navigating the city with two children, one of whom couldn't yet speak English, was a daily struggle, but now I look back on it as a comedy of errors. A petite, dark-haired young woman from the local news scurrying by the front desk of my building, the doorman greeting us as I struggled with Holly and made sure Lee Heh didn't venture too far ahead.

Then there was the relationship between the two girls. Lee Heh was clearly not a fan of Holly's outbursts and demonstrative behavior, but Holly was attached to her sister. She'd often call for Lee Heh to come sleep with her, over Lee Heh's objections. Naturally, as the mother, I'd try to referee some type of compromise where we could all give a little for the good of the family.

I got the chance to investigate their past when a literary agent called after seeing a TV interview with me and Lee Heh talking about international adoption.

"Hi, I'm Bill Adler, and I think you've got a book in you," he said.

"You do? Is that something you can help with?" I asked.

"I certainly can."

I loved the idea. It was clear by the number of media requests that there was a lot of interest in the topic. A book would give people a better understanding of the process and encourage others to adopt. After receiving my marching orders, I got to work on the project and wrote several hundred pages about my experience. The publisher loved it but wanted me to return to Korea and Vietnam for more research and possibly even contact some of the girls' family members.

"Bill, I think it's a wonderful idea. I've already created a draft of over 300 pages, but I simply can't travel right now. I've got my hands full with my job and taking care of the children."

"I have an idea," he said. "I know an author and journalist who might be able to help."

Soon, Bill had introduced me to a woman named Ruth Gruber. She had already written an impressive array of well-researched books, and she was willing to travel abroad.

In June of 1974, Ruth returned from Asia after fulfilling her mission to research the girls' pasts. She'd taken along her daughter, Celia Michaels, a lovely, talented woman who handled the photography. The information they had collected about Lee Heh and Holly went into the book but also helped me as I tried to teach them how to blend their pasts with their present so they could confidently reach for the future.

The best thing they brought us were pictures. Pictures of Lee Heh's brothers. A picture of Lee Heh with her mother and father. So much about Lee Heh fell into place: her refusal to speak Korean, her fear of my father's Korean friends, and her terror of being abandoned by me unless she was a perfect child.

Lee Heh was eight months old when her father died. She and her two brothers lived with their mother who sewed and cleaned to keep her small family together. The mother contracted tuberculosis. Lee Heh had been placed in an orphanage and her files were misplaced. She was mistakenly sent to another orphanage for adoption. When her mother and brothers returned to the orphanage, they were informed of the transfer. After much talk, and a lot of tears, they decided since the mother was dying, it would be best for Lee Heh to be adopted. So, out of love, they gave her up. When we were trying to find them, they were trying to find us, and our paths crossed.

Lee Heh had buried her memories as a way to survive. When she came home from school, we told her what Ruth had learned and showed her the pictures. She identified her brothers by name. She wanted to stay and talk, but she had promised a friend she would go to her party. As she left, she hugged me. "I'll hurry home. I want to hear about my brothers and my mother."

Then Ruth informed me about Holly. I knew Holly had been traumatized, but not to the full extent. Ruth discovered that Holly had almost been adopted once before, but the person who found her for her friend noticed red scars on Holly's wrist. She realized Holly had been mistreated and she was not interested in an "abused" child. Ruth confirmed my feelings that Holly had experienced physical trauma.

She also brought me pictures for Holly. They were in an album which had been a present from the woman we were fairly sure was Holly's mother. There were pictures of Holly as an infant, toddler, and young child. From Ruth I also learned that Holly's life had run the gamut, from relative wealth to extreme poverty. Holly had to learn to fight or be destroyed. *Holly*, I thought, *how much can I tell you? You're just beginning to take hold.*

Ruth encouraged me to show her the pictures immediately. But I wondered if they would bring her back to a past that had been so full of turmoil that she wouldn't be able to handle it. Eventually, I acquiesced and showed her the photos. She looked at them and made comments. Then she hugged the album. Holly now had an identity to cling to.

CHAPTER 4

Motherhood's Delicate Balance

Toughness doesn't have to come in a pinstripe suit.
– DIANE FEINSTEIN

IN 1975, WHEN I WAS ASSIGNED to cover that Vietnam Baby Lift story, I went to Washington to interview a number of government officials. Ed Mezvinsky was one of those people. I immediately found him to be warm and intriguing. Ed was curious when I told him about my daughters. A lot of the interview centered around them. He was dear, sweet, and open. "If he ever calls, I'm going to marry him," I thought. And that was a first for me. To this day, I'm still not sure if that meeting was a blessing or a burden, probably a bit of both, but we'll get to that.

As I was leaving the office, he looked at me. "Would you like to have dinner tonight?"

"That would be a treat," I replied.

Little did either of us know the ride we were about to take. We saw a lot of each other that weekend. Then he went on a trip to Russia. When he returned, we began to see each other frequently. Very soon, it was apparent we were going to be married. It was time for me to tell Lee Heh and Holly they were going to have to share their mother with another person. Not only her time, but their living space.

While looking at Ed and me, Holly fell into her role as troublemaker. When I told her that I was getting married to someone, she replied, "Is it Roger?" (a former boyfriend of mine). Despite that, Holly welcomed Ed easily and even asked if she could call him "Dad."

Lee Heh had a harder time with the news. When I told her Ed would be part of our family, she claimed that I had little credibility, pointing out that the last time I told her I was bringing someone home who she would enjoy, it was Holly. Admittedly, she had reason to be cautious.

Ed spent lots of quality time with the girls, and soon won them over. We were married on October 5th, 1975, and became a family of four, actually more than that. First, Lee Heh's brothers Kyoo Sik and Kyoo Bok had been located in Korea, and they arrived in the US on the same day as our wedding. Then, Ed had four daughters from his first marriage. They were 13, 11, 8, and 6, quite a range of ages, and that contributed greatly to the size of our brood. From the outset, all the girls were included in our outings. Early on, we became a family of six children. The girls spent many weekends with us, and I was quick to learn one of the great challenges of mothering once removed, stepmothering.

The same year, I asked to be transferred to Washington to be near Ed and accepted a position at WRC-TV, Channel 4, in Washington, DC, an NBC-owned station. I was at that station from 1975 until 1990 and was also a contributor to the *Today Show*.

Our family settled in the Kalorama area of the city, a tiny neighborhood known for its embassies, mansions, and many famous residents. We had a nice life there and the girls seemed to take to the city with more ease than they had in New York. Holly was sent to Georgetown Day which had a relaxed environment that suited her. She was quite popular in her elementary school with a gaggle of girls who seemed drawn to her outgoing nature. Lee Heh went to Cathedral School complete with uniforms and a more structured approach to learning. It was important for me to enroll them in the school that best suited them so they would feel at home in DC.

It wasn't long before our house became a place where neighbors, friends, business associates, and relatives dropped by, sometimes for a quick visit, and other times a much longer one. (That busy household foreshadowed what was to come.)

Here's a quick vignette of that time from my cousin, David Sostman.

> In 1974, imbued with a passion for history, politics, and the American story, I chose to attend college in Washington, DC. Political science and psychology were my academic areas, and they formed the lens through which I saw the world. I was lucky to study at George Washington University, and in my internships with a young senator from Delaware, and later in the Carter White House, I benefited from being able to watch history unfold in real-time.
>
> That perspective was undoubtably enhanced in 1976, when my cousin Marjorie asked if I would like to live in a basement apartment in the large Kalorama DC home that she, Ed, Lee Heh and Holly were moving into. That move marked my entry into what I referred to as the Margolies-Mezvinsky magic kingdom.
>
> Marjorie, at 34, and Ed at 39 were a young, attractive power couple whose marriage at the intersection of media and politics garnered considerable attention, which was fun

to observe. Lee Heh's adultlike manner that contrasted with Holly's canny urchin behavior and my own hippy-like disposition added to the joyful atmosphere, as did the occasional weekend presence of Ed's four young daughters from his earlier marriage. Marjorie's pregnancy and Marc's entry into the world in December 1977 took the energy and warmth to an even higher level as he became the focus of everyone's love.

Before Marc's birth there were two occasions in 1977 that served to encapsulate life in the Margolies-Mezvinsky magic circus. The first was an overnight visit from Marjorie's high school friends Kenny and Maxine, who at the time were producers of the successful Broadway Musical—Grease. I had met them previously and they were charming and fun to be around.

The same day Ed was scheduled to meet in the evening with Allard Lowenstein, the former congressman from New York who in 1968 orchestrated the "Dump Johnson" movement and encouraged Bobby Kennedy to run for President. Lowenstein was the current US Representative to the United Nations for Human Rights, a post originally held by Eleanor Roosevelt, and he was passing that position on to Ed, who was selected for that post by the Carter Administration after he lost his reelection to Congress the previous November. Ed asked me to join him, since among other things I was a WH Intern at the time and Human Rights was a primary focus of the Administration. As we were leaving the house to meet up with Lowenstein, Kenny, who knew Al and his reputation for long talks into the evening, said he'd bet money that Lowenstein would end up sleeping at the house.

We picked up Lowenstein at his hotel on New Hampshire Ave. in DC and after everyone else went to bed around 1:00 AM, he and I stayed up talking into the night until around 3:00, at which point he slept on the couch in the living room of my basement apartment. We got up a few hours later and I drove him to National Airport for an early morning flight—after he put my name in a notebook that he kept, which I later learned contained the names of hundreds of young men and women he had influenced. When he was shot in his NY law office three years later by a deranged former student of his from Stanford, thousands of idealistic hearts across the nation were broken by the loss of a man who had touched so many lives.

The other memorable occasion occurred in August 1977, when Elvis Presley died at the age of forty. In the media coverage that ensued, I was watching a newscast with Holly who was nine at the time, and after they showed his early appearances on the Ed Sullivan show and other perform-ances, she exclaimed, "Who is that? He's so cool!" That began her obsession with Elvis. His universal appeal hit her right in the heart, and she became an Elvis fan. Recognizing this, Marjorie asked someone at RCA/Columbia Records if they could send her a few Elvis records. They responded by sending her a large cardboard box containing dozens of Elvis albums produced through the years. Upon opening the box, Marjorie pulled out a few and gave them to Holly for her birthday, which made her ecstatic. She ran up to her room, put them on her Close and Play phonograph, and listened to them for hours. The box of records was then hidden in the back of a first-floor closet.

A few weeks later, Holly somehow found the complete box of hidden records. Later when we looked in her room a dozen or more of the classic Elvis record albums were out of their protective sleeves and strewn all over her bed and the floor while one was playing on her phonograph. I said to Marjorie, "It looks like she's had her first romantic crush—with Elvis."

We enjoyed being in the city, but decided to make another change, and that did not bode well for young Holly. We chose to move back to my home state to be near my parents and family and build our life there. I'd still be able to commute to DC for work, so we settled just outside of Philadelphia. Lee Heh adapted quickly, but this time Holly's transition was not as smooth.

Despite the machinations in my personal life, work was going gangbusters. I was nabbing great assignments and had access to the political powerhouses in the DMV area (DC, Maryland, and Virginia). Being a woman in a man's workplace came with its own challenges, but with persistence and dogged determination, I made a bit of a name for myself in the newsroom as the one who could break the ice with interviewees and get them to open up quickly, despite whatever news event they were navigating.

Maybe it was an offshoot of the mothering techniques I'd learned, but I was able to form a connection quickly, diffuse an interviewee's apprehension, and go in with the challenging questions...while getting it all on film. Each big story that I got in the can meant more professional exposure. It also served to prove to my boss that he could keep sending the women in the newsroom out on location with confidence.

Being a news reporter for a TV station was a great fit for me because every day was different and each assignment unique. That fed into my need for variety instead of a rigid daily routine. I've always enjoyed the surprises that each day brings, the promise of excitement on the other side of the dawn.

Sometimes I worked on an extended story assignment, but for the most part, I'd come to the office only to be greeted with a new lead, a breaking story that needed coverage. The crew and I would load into the news van, and I would have to become an expert on a particular topic during our ride to the location.

One of the most important things I learned was psychology and human behavior, how to read people and use their responses to get the information needed to tell the story. With the help of an editor, I also learned to edit film and use slides to create still images, how to write concise, clear copy, and how to measure and time every second of a story before it went to air.

For stories that lasted one minute and forty seconds on the evening news, I could spend over three hours filming with a cameraman or woman and a sound engineer. At times, I was submitting more than one a day, which meant driving to multiple locations, filming the stories, and then either reporting on location or rushing back to the studio to write copy and have all the editing done by 6:00. Then I'd get camera-ready so I could present the story live during the evening news.

I learned to approach the stories about children cautiously because I had no idea where they would lead: lighthearted human interest story angle or worse, much, much worse. But I had no choice since I was the go-to in the newsroom for everything from family tragedy to feel-good fluff pieces. When a story came in that involved a child, it never failed that I'd hear, "That's a Marjorie story" from a chorus of men in the newsroom. But there were also some big breaks, and that's when the job became truly exciting.

One night in 1978, I was having a dinner party at our home when the phone rang. It was the news station. "There's a story unfolding, and we need someone to cover it."

"I'd love to help," I said, "but I'm actually hosting a party right now. If you can't find anyone else, call me back."

Maybe ten minutes later, the phone rang again. I apologized to our guests and excused myself. I had to go with a film crew to Vienna, Virginia. There was a missing kid, a boy. His name was Billy Viscidi. Fortunately for me, the family had just relocated from New York, and they recognized me from my TV job there. That helped them warm up to me because they weren't talking to many other reporters. Luckily, they trusted me on the spot.

I could see this huge story unfolding before my eyes. It was just the luck of the draw, but it turned out to be a dream assignment, one that journalists live for. The family invited me inside their home while other reporters sat on the ground outside, and they were such kind people. It's rare for a television reporter to be handed a story like that and I was ready to run with it. The police even called me with information about the case since I was so closely connected to the family.

The police also played the tapes of the brother's questioning for me because they knew the family was confiding in me. Then my interviews hit a wall. The family clammed up because they felt I was betraying them by reporting updates to the story.

The older brother, Larry, was put on trial, but the charges were eventually dismissed. The saga ended on a sad note as the twelve-year-old boy was found in a shallow grave in the family's backyard nineteen days after he went missing. He had died of a fractured skull and his body was in a plastic bag in the vegetable garden.

A month after the body was found, fifteen-year-old Larry confessed to a psychologist, who hypnotized him and administered truth serum, that he had killed his brother. He had blocked the traumatic event from his mind. It was truly a sensational story that held the community's attention for months as details gradually began to unfold.

I could tell right away that first night that others thought it would be important because there were several reporters from the same media outlet on location. It was unusual for TV stations to send more than one reporter for a story. I certainly didn't "own" the story, but I did find myself at the center of it because of the unprecedented access that the family gave me. That scoop landed me on the cover of *Washingtonian* magazine with a feature story on my experiences during the high-profile case.

Later, I was on a radio show talking about the story when a

call came in. We were just about to wrap up when she identified herself as Grace Viscidi. I talked to her on the air and then later she and her husband Burton agreed to an exclusive five-part interview that I would host on News Center 4.

Other stories were more lighthearted, titillating even. There was one series titled "Mistresses." The copy was written with a salacious tilt to entice viewers. "In Washington, it happens a lot. In a city filled with money and power...love triangles have become part of everyday life. Marjorie Margolies takes a sensitive look at the women who are caught up in these affairs, how they live, and the emotions they share."

While I enjoyed the lighthearted fare for a change of pace, most were as tragic as the Viscidi story. With each assignment, I tried to present the information with as much sensitivity as possible, but it was important to inform the public of the dangers that existed. I did an eight-part series on sexual abuse called "The Crying Shame." It was difficult and heart-wrenching, with many of the interviewees choosing to keep their faces hidden and their voices disguised.

Then there was a five-part series called "They Have No Voice," which also focused on the sexual abuse of children. I won several awards for that series including one called the Golden Mike for America's Best Local Television Programs in the Interest of Youth.

I powered through those stories because it was my job, but each time I had to review photos from the morgue or see evidence of injuries at the hospital, it only served to crush my spirit. It was unimaginable to me, someone who had begun a family through adoption, that children were treated this way in the most advanced country in the world.

I did not only have to go on location to film the gruesome details; I then had to go back to the newsroom to prepare it, and next present it on the air as professionally as I could, reliving it each time. So, my entire day was consumed with the horrors that befell those young lives. They were some of the toughest days for me. With most stories, I could compartmentalize them, almost like I was watching from above, seeing myself performing the job at a safe emotional distance. But when they involved children, I was never able to remove myself. They just reminded me too much of my own children because our family was growing so quickly.

One day out of the blue, Nancy Bennett called and asked if we would take a "hard to place" Vietnamese family. There were four Has, a mother, a father and two children. I turned to Ed and asked, "What about four more?"

"Sure," he said.

The Has were the first of a number of families who lived with us. Mrs. Suu, her son, Vu, her two nephews, and later her husband joined us and stayed for 25 years. Yes, 25 years!

On December 10, 1977, when Marc, our first "bio-child" was born, there was a lot of change in a short period of time as the chorus of children's voices grew and filled our house for years to come. Sometimes, when the din became too great, I'd stare at the ceiling and remind myself, "Careful what you wish for."

But of course, I wouldn't have changed a thing.

CHAPTER 5

No Place Like Home

The family unit plays a critical role in our society and in the
training of the generation to come.

– SANDRA DAY O'CONNOR

IN 1980, ED CAME BURSTING THROUGH the front door with an exuberance I'd rarely seen from him. "I just drove by a house that is perfect for us," he said with a grin.

"A house?" I asked. "Where is it? Is it big enough for all of us?"

"Yes, it needs some work, it's something of a white elephant, but I think it's the perfect place to raise a growing family. Our growing family."

"That certainly sounds ideal," I said.

When we first drove up to the historic Colonial together, I saw the arched roof, the stonework, the flourish of plants, and it caused a visceral reaction inside me. I loved growing up in my parent's house, but since I'd been out on my own, I'd never seen my homes as anything more than a temporary place to stay.

I didn't think in the long term because with my job there was always the possibility of relocating. Even when Ed and I got the house in Washington, DC, it simply fulfilled a need. It was beautiful, well-located, and served us well, but it wasn't "home."

So, when I got out of the car and stood in front of the house that Ed had found, that feeling caught me off guard. I agreed with his assessment of the towering house. I had become used to the higher DC real estate prices, so the more affordable price sealed the deal. We were soon homeowners of the estate said to have been modeled after the thatched farmhouse of Anne Hathaway, wife of William Shakespeare, that was built over 500 years ago.

By the time we'd finished the renovation, the 1929 stone house, which sat on over two secluded acres, had six bedrooms, four and a half bathrooms, and almost 7,300 square feet of living space. I was enamored by the charm and period details like the cathedral ceilings, stone fireplaces, exotic hardwood flooring, gourmet kitchen, and Juliet balcony in the primary bedroom. There was even a ballroom complete with Belgian marble tile floors that we used for political functions and dinners as well as making the space available to local charities.

Other immigrant families needing temporary shelter stayed in the pool house until the Suu family arrived and set up camp. It took us a while to get used to Mrs. Suu and her quirks. First, she didn't speak English, and then she refused to shake the cultures and ways of her homeland. For example, when Andrew was a toddler and she was in charge of watching him, she'd encourage him to pee on the gardenias in the living room. The plants needed to be watered, and Mrs. Suu was sure the acid would help them flourish. So, anytime someone walked past the living room early in the morning, they were likely to see a small boy sidled up to one of the planters with his pants on the floor. Maybe she was onto something because visitors always commented on our gorgeous gardenias. I would just smile.

Mrs. Suu loved to cook, and I suppose as a way of integrating herself into the family when she first arrived, she asked Ed (the "head of the house" in her mind) what he liked to eat. When he said that he enjoyed chicken, she prepared a lovely feast. Then she proceeded to cook chicken for dinner almost every night for the next several years. It became so frequent that when Holly came downstairs for dinner, she'd start flapping her arms. "Bawk, bawk!"

Clearly, with such a large house, a burgeoning family, and demanding careers, we would need some help. I quickly placed an ad in the local newspaper classifieds that read:

Mary Poppins, where are you?
Live-in person or couple needed to love kids, clean, drive,
and cook for a large family. Separate quarters. Refs. Req'd.

The position was filled a few times over the years, with varying degrees of success. Susan, the first one, was a lovely person and quite stylish. She actually showed up to the interview with an umbrella in hand, a la Mary Poppins. Then there was Margarita who was so stylish that sometimes people thought that she was the mother and I the nanny.

We had another who was somewhat prickly. She forbade us from entering the kitchen when she was preparing meals. Then there was Delores, a funny, lanky, Cruella DeVille-type who smoked like a chimney and even slipped a few cigarettes to a couple of the children. She'd also show up to work with jewelry and coats that looked exactly like the ones I'd misplaced. (I think I could write a book entitled *Maids I Have Worked For*.)

Irene Lane, of the Lane Montessori School, has her own memories of the Margolies-Mezvinsky family.

As a Montessori Preschool Administrator, there I was sitting at my desk as usual, waiting to greet the next set of parents and child for fall enrollment. I hear the customary knock at my door, and I raise my eyes to see two women holding hands with a very small Vietnamese boy. I remember this boy was so tiny and his little legs so skinny. His Vietnamese mom just there on one side, holding that small child tightly to her leg as they moved forward into the chairs almost as one being. Marjorie introduces me to Mrs. Suu and Vu. She is beaming with pride as she shares Vu's story and that of his mother. She shared a vision in a way that was contagious.

There are these rare moments where life is changed forever. If one were to ponder God's will that day, she spoke his words into my ears and a whole world opened up into what every human being can do for every other human being. That was her message. That was the new world available. Not only was I a 'YES!' but Lane Montessori School gave Vu a full scholarship!

Now 45 years later, with grey hair and a wrinkled, happy smile, I remember back to those early Marjorie years. She would later enroll Marc and Andrew when they were old enough and our friendship grew from there.

That house turned out to be the perfect place to raise our kids and entertain family, friends, and associates. Some of my favorite times were at night when everyone was still, the lights dimmed, and the curtains drawn. I'd sit in the courtyard near the pool and listen as the chirps of the frogs signaled the end to another day. Sometimes, I'd be so comfortable as the breeze swirled around the pool so gently that I'd take a quick nap, but those respites were rare.

They say it takes a village, and I suppose we were creating our own in that secluded stone house. At one time, we housed a truly multicultural family that included a Vietnamese family, our Jewish bio-kids, an African American live-in, and a Canadian handyman who drove the kids to their appointments when we couldn't be there. We had our own little melting pot where everyone felt comfortable and welcomed.

In one instance, Ed's daughter was living with us while she went to school. When she left for college, we maintained her room for visits during school breaks. I was doing a story on a young man who had been adjudicated to the Glen Mills Reform School and had gone on to athletic prominence. He then returned to Philly to compete in the shot put during the Penn Relays, an annual track and field competition that began way back in 1895.

I had actually spoken at his high school graduation, and I remember his elation in being accepted to Dartmouth with the highest college boards in the history of the school at that time. During the shot-put event, he had made two attempts that were shockingly abysmal but on his third try, he paused, focused, and made the winning throw. That ability to overcome obstacles was symbolic of most things in his life and that was the focus of my news story.

While interviewing him, I found out he was on a break from school and had nowhere to stay, so of course he ended up with us at Chateau Margolies-Mezvinsky. Ed's daughter came home from school expecting to find her room as she left it...and she did. Except for the fact that a large, muscular local athlete had now taken over.

That was not the exception but the rule. With an ever-changing cast of characters, it was difficult to keep track of who was staying there at any one time. We have a friend who joked that someone could drop off a dog for pet sitting when she went on vacation, and we'd never know the difference. I can tell you that did happen!

There was always a basketball game going on outside, maybe a meeting in the ballroom, or a party by the pool, often at the same time. I suppose others may shudder at the idea of having so many people around, but to me the house was hectic, confusing, exciting, and bursting with life.

If we were involved in a political campaign at the time, the number of people coming by would swell as the election approached. Then it would subside until the next cycle. The major benefit of that for our children was that they interacted with so many people from all walks of life that they learned how to get along with just about anyone.

There were certainly unusual circumstances. At one time, the 1960s folk music group Peter, Paul, and Mary were singing "Puff the Magic Dragon" in our ballroom for a fundraiser. Another time, I went to pick up actress and humanitarian Audrey Hepburn from the airport with Marc and Andrew in the backseat because I didn't have a sitter.

At one point, Ed and I took Marc, Vu, and Andrew to Florida for an event we had to attend. Then the plan was to take the boys to Disneyworld. While we were gone, one of the girls had planned a modest pool party. Before we made it to the Magic Kingdom, we got a call from a concerned parent saying that there had been a raid at our house and over 200 teenagers were arrested. Somehow, word had spread, and the small pool party ended up attracting hundreds of rambunctious teenagers. The story made the local papers, and to this day people approach me to say, "I remember when my child got arrested at your house." Oops!

Around that time, I also managed to take a trip to Korea. Fifteen years after I had picked Lee Heh up at the O'Hare Airport when she first arrived in the U.S., she was meeting me at the Seoul National Airport. For her junior semester, she had been studying at Yonsei University in Korea. I decided to join her after the semester was over. Before I arrived, I had told her that NBC News would like to send a crew with me, and *People* magazine was also interested in doing a story. I asked, "Do you mind if they come along?" She said, "No, that would be fun." She was interested in journalism.

Our first several days together were spent catching up. Lee Heh showed me where she had studied. The only images I had of Yonsei University were the ones I'd seen on the news. In April of 1985, Yonsei had been the site of many student demonstrations. As a mother, seeing those pictures on the television screen each night gave me cause for concern.

By the time I arrived, most of the students had already left for their summer break so the campus was quiet. There had been a number of protests, and I could still smell the tear gas that permeated the school. Lee Heh and I talked. We shopped. She accompanied me to a speech. I met her friends who even helped us get through an interview with a Korean television station because *They Came to Stay* had been translated into Korean through *Reader's Digest Condensed Books*.

Since I was single at the time of adoption, that topic was of special interest there, we were told, because Koreans rarely adopted and single adoptions were unheard of. It was for that reason our story was the focus of some attention. For us, the tours, the sights, the shopping and even the interviews were all quite secondary. Our main purpose was to learn about Lee Heh's past, to visit the orphanage she came from...to go back.

After I returned to the news station in Washington, we began reviewing the footage and working on the story that would air. Joe, the editor who I was working with, said, "We've got to get an interview with Lee Heh to finish the story."

"No way," I said. "I'm not going to do that. This has already been more intrusive than I had anticipated."

We continued reviewing the hours and hours of raw footage,

and then, at the very end of the reel, Joe said, "Look at this."

There was Lee Heh on film being interviewed. The cameraman had apparently asked his own questions to her during some downtime. I couldn't believe it. That had never happened to me before.

"This is exactly what the story needs," Joe said.

In hindsight, I would have never allowed the media to join us if I'd known the story angle would end up being so personal to Lee Heh and me. It was my impression that the focus would be on the American adoptions that had taken place using me, a woman who had a successful adoption, as an example. However, Lee Heh's contribution was quite moving. Below was how the piece turned out, with my narration.

> [Lee Heh] *I really don't remember anything about this place at all. I don't remember the people or where I stayed or the way I felt. So, it was a whole new experience coming back. It's as if I was never here. It's just kind of strange.*
>
> *It kind of hit me that I was finally back here, where I'd come from. When I was adopted, I was around six years old, and I think I was here [the orphanage] for about six months. I was fortunate that I wasn't here too long. It was a whole new experience coming back. It's as if I was never here.*
>
> [Marjorie] *"Here" was the Harry Holt Memorial Chapel. In the chapel with us were 40 members of a group called The Motherland Tour. All Korean adoptees brought up in the United States. There in Korea, like Lee Heh, in search of their identities.*
>
> *The tour was sponsored by the Holt Children's Services Agency. Bertha Holt and her husband Harry had started it all in 1955. They had six children and then adopted six more Korean orphans. They'd bought land close to the demilitarized zone, land that no one else wanted.*

[Lee Heh] *It finally hit me that I was here, back where I'd come from, and it just made me realize how lucky I am.*

[Marjorie] *I knew Lee Heh's biological father had died when she was just a year old, and her mother contracted tuberculosis. She was too sick to care for Lee Heh and later the mother died. Lee Heh had gotten her aunt's number and address many years ago, but we were told her aunt had moved. Luckily with help and a lot of persistence, we were able to track her down. Lee Heh's only living relative in Korea, her link to the past.*

In Inchon, Korea, Kim Chong Young, her husband, and three boys lived in a modest apartment complex. The first thing we saw were pictures of Lee Heh and her two brothers. They came to America five years after Lee Heh and were adopted by another family. We kept in touch with them and have watched them marry and have children of their own.

It was time to address unanswered questions.

"What was my mother like?" Lee Heh asked.

"She had a pretty face," the aunt responded.

"Was she tall, short, smart? Did she have brothers and sisters?"

"Your mother was very sick. She was 37 when she died. You had been gone for a year."

"What was my father like?" Lee Heh wondered.

"He died when you were just a year old. We are incredibly grateful for what your American mother has done for you."

"I love my American mother very much," Lee Heh said softly.

At the end of the trip, Lee Heh summed it up. "I wouldn't say I've found my entire identity. That will probably take a lifetime, but I'd say I found a part of it."

After each trip, I was glad to get home to the family, but Holly wasn't always a fan of the constant buzz of energy that emanated from the old stone house. She said, "I hated having friends over. I hated getting picked up from school because I never knew what and who was going to show up. I hated going out to dinner or on vacation because we were such showstoppers, a caravan of circus freaks. Our sheer mass attracted such attention, not to mention its various personalities and languages...growing up in the Margolies-Mezvinsky household had the subtleties of a livestock auction. There was constant noise, random traffic of family, friends, and complete strangers; some came with cameras and microphones, others with pens and pads. *People* and *The Inquirer* wanted to know how Marjorie and Ed did it all! Not me. Because I desperately wanted to be 'normal.'"

One of Holly's famous flareups had quite an effect on me. I forget the details, but I wrote her a really long letter stressing that while I didn't like her behavior, I would always be there for her, would always love her, and that everybody felt that way about her even if she didn't believe any of it.

I can still see the letter, carefully written on a yellow notepad, outlining each issue that we had been encountering and putting it in a positive light. I'd slid the letter under her door and a bit later I walked into her bathroom and looked down. There were shards of yellow paper strewn all over the floor around the wastebasket. I had to steady myself against the vanity as I looked at the mess she had made. It was her way of punishing me. It felt so devastating because regardless of how hard I tried, I couldn't get her to understand that no matter what she did, and I mean no matter WHAT she did, I would be there for her.

I had to learn to accept the fact that when Holly got angry or frustrated or annoyed, she'd go into this dark hole and was convinced that was where she belonged. There was no rescuing her despite my motherly urge to do just that. When she was a teenager, I received a phone call one night from a woman who I later learned was in jail with a murder charge. She told me my daughter had been arrested and needed bail money. I could hear Holly in the background yelling, "I love you, Mom!" She had been caught buying cocaine with her friends.

Then I began putting together the pieces, which I had to do often to make sense of her stories. A few weeks prior, we had driven by a corner in West Philly, and she said out of the blue, "Kids buy drugs there all the time," pointing out the window. "No one ever gets arrested because the cops just look the other way." I thought that was such an oddly specific thing to mention, but just brushed it off as one of Holly's attempts at saying something shocking. Then it turned out that's where she had been arrested.

When I picked her up, she was wearing an unusual outfit, a white t-shirt with the neck around her waist like a skirt, then another white t-shirt for a top. Her face looked drawn and tired, old makeup caked on from the night before, and there was dried blood on her legs. Apparently, she and her friends had driven to that very corner she'd pointed out to me earlier and ended up purchasing coke from an undercover cop. Since she was the one driving the car and she had handed the police officer the money, they arrested her and let her friends go. They had the whole sting operation on video.

That was bad enough on its own, but at the time, Ed was running for Attorney General and one of his talking points was the devastating role drugs were playing on the destruction of our community. The arrest didn't immediately make the news because she was "Holly Margolies" and he was "Ed Mezvinsky."

After she was prosecuted and ultimately sentenced with a fine and six months of probation, Ed held a press conference and made it clear that we were like any other family dealing with teenagers who get in trouble. We wanted her to be treated just like anyone else who broke the law to show how drugs were affecting all families. We were facing the same difficulties and concerns as so many others in Philadelphia and across the country.

I have to admit that even when Holly was most challenging, I could see improvement. It was very obvious to me that she was getting better, but it could be frustrating when she didn't take advantage of her opportunities. She was good in school, she was good on the field, and her school reports were always positive... when she was happy. If Holly liked a school subject, she would do great, but if she didn't like it, things went downhill fast. She'd usually pass her classes because she knew she had to get to the other side, but her full potential often wasn't realized.

Holly got into Smith and didn't apply to the University of Pennsylvania (my alma mater) despite my urging because she didn't think she could get in. Lee Heh had applied to Brown and Penn for early admission and got into both. One of the questions on the admissions for Penn was something like "If you were stuck on a desert island, who would you want to be with?" Lee Heh wrote a beautiful essay about how she would like to be there with her biological mother and ended by quoting the poem *The Answer (To an Adopted Child)* by Fleur Conkling Heyliger.

Four years later, Lee Stetson, the dean of admissions at Penn, agreed to meet with me and Holly, I think, partially because they had wanted Lee Heh to attend but she had chosen Brown. I also learned that Lee and his wife had adopted an Asian child.

Holly could be such a charmer when she wanted to be. She had a way of going into survival mode to get what she needed. For the Penn interview, she was funny, personable, and quite impressive. Lee seemed taken with her and advised her to do well at Smith and then transfer to Penn, which she did.

She had enjoyed her first year at Smith but decided to take his advice and transfer. Once she began at Penn, she succumbed to temptation and spent most of her time partying. My approach to her behavior was to tell her, "This isn't who you are. It's how you've chosen to behave." After her second year there, she decided to take a gap year and reassess her plans. She promised to finish school and she did.

As the youngest, my son Andrew Mezvinsky (who is currently an artist living in Austria) was one of the last of the children to live in the house, and he has vivid memories of those years in Penn Valley, Pennsylvania.

I was the youngest of the kids in the family, so I had lots of brothers and sisters to play with. Our home was a communal environment with a lot of people going in and out of the house. We were fostering other families and providing a place where people could change their lives and situations. That environment gave me a foundation in which I understood there was a safety net with a solid family structure.

When friends were over, my sister, Holly, would ask if we could adopt any of them. It was always an open environment. I moved to the city at around 12 to live with my grandmother. I knew that I wanted to be an artist by the age of 8. For me, once I was away and got my own space, I saw that I needed that because it gave me a sense of independence.

I received a lot of attention as the youngest. I was also forgotten about at times, so I experienced those extremes. I was the king of hand-me-downs and didn't buy my own clothes until I went to university. Teachers knew my mom and dad by name, so I chose to go to high school in the inner city with a large African American population. There, fewer people knew who my parents were.

Knowing you have those figureheads, you're careful being a teenager. Having my sister on the front page of the Inquirer *for a house party meant I couldn't be a fuck up. Any little slip might be seen by a reporter who would write a story. That wouldn't just be bad for me but my family as well. I graduated from high school at 16 and went to university in Scotland.*

Because there were always so many different types of people in our house, it taught me that I could speak to anyone, from an ambassador to an organ donor, it ran the gamut. My mother knew how hard it was to be an artist. Having a normal income was difficult enough so they wanted to lean me toward architecture, but I was headstrong. There was no right or wrong answer.

The example my parents set built a work ethic in me. I wanted to be involved in the conversation on an intellectual level, continuously asking questions. Mom was in DC more, and Dad was around the house. Mrs. Suu, Vu's mother, was the one who helped me out on the day to day. My mom and dad were there when I needed them, but they were also working parents. They were involved in helping the community. Dad was at every track event I was in because he had run track himself. When I had an art show, they were there, but never hovering parents.

One thing that's stuck with me as far as my mother's advice was "you can never please everybody" and "there's sometimes no right answer." Look at a problem or find a problem that you think you can solve. There's a way of dealing with people where there's an understanding that they need to be heard so that you can grasp how you can help and what you can do.

Some things she imparted were based on her actions, what she did for other people, and connecting human beings and seeing the good that it did gave me the understanding that I needed to live life simply so others can simply live. It was difficult for me to understand as a child that when as kids we would ask for something, Mom would say, "Do you need it, or do you want it?" and make it a philosophical discussion.

In life, you usually don't get a yes or no. The big thing she taught me was that if you can help others, then do it. It was the idea of being generous with your shelter and what you can offer. The best thing was the communal family unit.

Lee Heh really helped raise me. She was an amazing support in the family structure. She was specific in how she talked, very to the point. She has a shaman-like, peaceful quality. It was a time when I knew she was a very significant part of my life.

I've lived in places like Mongolia with nomads, with no water and electricity, and my family helped prep me for that. There were always lots of books around the house. Occasionally, Lee Heh would bring up a book and say it changed her life. Of course, I'd read it, and it was her point of view at that time. She taught me to be practical about my life and realize I had to come back to reality. She always reminded me to be grounded after travel and creating artwork. Now, when I make it to the US, I always visit her and try to go around the country to see all my family.

Holly and Lee Heh were very different. Lee Heh was about responsibility. Holly was like, "Enjoy life. Have fun, do things within normalcy, don't overdo, but enjoy your life. Don't let anyone hold you back." She exuded a sense of energy, like a prankster, but someone who had no malice. She was always joking. When she would go into her room, everyone wanted to be around her because she was so goofy.

Holly was experimental when it came to expanding her mind. As a teenager when I got into trouble, it was nice having someone like her who had gone through it before. Being the last one in the house, she saw that it could be an emptiness for me. What Holly brought to the family was a kind of humor, sometimes dark, but always in a manner that was genuinely funny. She had an essence where she knew how to make you laugh. "If the boys think I'm cute, I'm going to shave my head." She had this internal confidence about her. I think it came from her mother and the story of her coming to the US. It gave her a strength that she carried herself with.

My brother Marc is four years older, and I looked up to him. I was into very different things. His room was littered with Jimi Hendrix paraphernalia, and he was into philosophy. I wanted to go to Spain and visit the Prado for my bar mitzvah. For his, Marc asked for a Roth IRA.

When Marc was a kid, he was already an overachiever, going through books quickly. His friends were always the funniest kids, also very laid back, just like him. He came out of the family situation as someone who is comfortable with anyone, and he's super smart. When he got to Stanford and studied religion and philosophy, he wanted to figure out how to make it a vocational option. He also liked numbers, playing with the ones and the zeroes.

Vu, Dang, and Hai are the fantastic Pham nation. Vu has an innocence and inquisitive nature about him. He's a few years older than Marc. They kind of included me with their friends, and a lot of Vu's friends in high school were the same age as Marc. So, they often hung out together. Vu never, ever felt like he was out of place. He felt like he had two moms and two dads. He has such a warm nature that you can talk to him, and it will always be pleasant. If Vu wasn't Vietnamese, he'd be Irish because he has the gift of gab. Dang would call me "troublemaker," and sometimes get me booze. He moved to California to do his own thing. Hai is also an all-around good guy.

At first my parents were surprised when I went into art because I was good at sports and asked to try out for different teams. When I told them that I wanted to go to a different school in the city that didn't offer sports, they were shocked. My grandmother was against it because she knew how hard an art career could be, but I've never looked back.

Since this is *my* book, I feel justified in adding my own quick story about Andrew. There was a Back-to-School event of his that I was unable to attend because I was casting a vote in Congress. Working parents understand this conundrum quite well. I just couldn't get out of my work obligation! But I knew that Ed and a couple of the children would be there to support him.

After that, all I heard from Andrew was, "Why didn't you come to my event?" "How could you miss it?" "Remember when you missed my Back-to-School night?"

In 1993, the Phillies were in the World Series, and as a member of Congress, I was given the opportunity to buy tickets that were impossible to get. I jumped at the chance and presented them to Andrew. As I held the tickets out in front of him, he reached for them, and I pulled them back.

"First, repeat after me. 'Mommy couldn't come to my Back-to-School night, but she was able to get me tickets to see the Phillies in the playoffs.'" He had a wonderful time at the game despite their loss.

Like any family, we experienced great excitement and crushing sorrow in our magical family home. It was the house in the neighborhood where the door was always open, and all were welcome.

My friend and neighbor Sue Rubel had three children. Her two oldest were out on their own, but a fourteen-year-old still lived with her. If he came home to an empty house, she instructed him to "go to the Margolies-Mezvinsky house. The door is never locked, and no one will notice another kid around the crowded dinner table." She had a point.

She also remembers, "Another guy had just moved in. Free room and board in exchange for maintenance, handywork, painting, garden etc. He told me, 'I'm really good at laying tile. Oh yeah, I can install new kitchen cabinets, too.'"

"Later, I had the chance to inspect his work. He did the job... kind of. Most of the cabinets stayed where he put them, but the floors dipped dangerously, and the ceiling fell down just a bit over the crooked island. All this while Mrs. Suu squatted over her chopped vegetables in preparation for dinner."

"Later, I heard that he thought 'in exchange for' included all the household silver as he fled the scene in the dead of night."

Like I said, it was not-so-controlled chaos, but for my generation, a house was a place to grow together, a symbol of success, a goal that had been reached. Every time I pulled into the driveway, it served as a reminder of all that we'd worked for and what we had achieved. That stone house with its sturdy walls and arched roof sheltered us from the elements for over two decades, and I never took it for granted.

CHAPTER 6

Politics Is a Blood Sport

*A woman is like a tea bag, you can't tell how strong she is
until you put her in hot water.*

– NANCY REAGAN

"THE YEAR OF THE WOMAN." I'm not sure how many times that phrase has been written and uttered, but it's ridiculous to me that the playing field is so uneven that it is necessary. When Hillary Clinton was on the verge of winning the 2016 election (which she should have won), the phrase was often bandied about. More recently, 2018 saw an unprecedented number of women not only running for Congressional offices but winning. Again, the Year of the Woman.

Probably the most well-known use of that term happened in 1992 when the Democratic stars aligned and over 100 women were elected to national office. There were 103 to be exact, and it was quite meaningful for me because I was one of those who won an election.

Those wins were partly fueled by the frustration women felt over the dismissal of sexual harassment allegations against then

Supreme Court nominee Clarence Thomas by Anita Hill. House members had even organized a march to the Senate to bring attention to the all-male Senate Judiciary Committee preparing to proceed with the nomination.

Then there was President George H.W. Bush who, when asked about The Year of the Woman, famously stated, "This is supposed to be the year of the women in the Senate...I hope a lot of them lose." That statement may have garnered him favor in his own party, but it also gave women voters the motivation to show up in record numbers. But I'm getting ahead of myself, which I tend to do.

It was never my intention to run for political office. My professional ambitions had been fulfilled as a busy reporter for NBC and its owned and operated stations. I had a demanding public-facing job, a sprawling home with an ever-changing number of occupants, and a husband who had held political office and continued to be active in local and national politics. So, in my mind, he was the politician in the family, and typically, one is more than enough.

However, in 1991, a steady buzz began to circle my orbit. Wherever I went, someone would utter a similar sentiment. Maybe it was because I had a bit of name recognition from TV, spent a lot of time in Washington, and was married to a politician, but it wasn't long before the attention was undeniable. It was always some form of the same question, "Would you consider running in the primary for the seat as the democratic candidate for the House?"

After much thought and consulting with Ed, I decided that it would be an interesting direction to pursue, but I also knew I'd have to leave reporting. Still, it was an opportunity that I just couldn't pass up. It would also show my children that I was willing to live up to one of my favorite mottos: "You can't win if you're not prepared to lose." So, I tossed my hat into the ring and officially entered the race.

Not too long after that, Representative Robert Lawrence Coughlin announced that he was retiring, leaving an open seat in the House of Representatives. That meant the winner of the primary wouldn't have to run against the incumbent but would face off against the Republican challenger. (As an interesting aside, women historically have a better chance of winning an open seat.)

Was it a sign of confidence that they thought I could win, or did they need a lamb to lead to the slaughter? The political battle would take place in Montgomery County, PA, an area that was a Republican stronghold; in fact, they were favored 2-to-1 over Democrats. To paint a better picture, a Democrat had not won an election in that district since 1916! So, what chance would a female Democratic neophyte have?

After I was approached by the Montgomery County Democratic Committee, I felt that if others saw that potential in me, the least I could do was follow through. I'd been taking chances throughout my life, so why should this be any different? Like everything I do, my first step was performing the necessary due diligence. I needed to conduct some research, find out exactly what I'd be getting myself into.

We'd hosted many political functions and gatherings at the house during my husband's career, so I decided to invite some of the local Democratic Club members to our home for what we called "girls sitting on the sofa," a casual collection of like-minded ladies hoping to find a candidate, preferably female, who could at least make a respectable showing.

I met many of the women over the next few weeks, including Arlene Halpern, a prominent member of the community. I asked Arlene what she remembers about those early gatherings.

When I met Marjorie, I was impressed with her energy and her bright personality. I connected with her immediately. I'd heard of her, of course, but we hadn't met. I liked that she was so warm and engaging. She had a sparkle and was extremely optimistic, which was the type of candidate we needed. Everyone was impressed.

Then I found out later, she had called my husband to say that she and I were going to be working together on this project and he should be prepared. That was typical Marjorie, always ahead of the game. It was just as well because things began to move quickly.

The next thing I know, I was holding a meeting in my own house and then more and more people were getting involved. It took off very quickly and fit in nicely with 'the year of the woman' theme. She just seemed like she was going to be the right person. She was eager and willing, which was wonderful.

Some of the Kennedys were known around that time for hosting afternoon teas. I decided to set up our own version of that. We called them evening coffee meetings where we could discuss the campaign and share our ideas. I would get a list of women and I didn't even have to twist anybody's arm. Everybody wanted to meet at that beautiful house for a serving of coffee and politics. It just kept mushrooming. We also had some big fundraising events and lots of intimate gatherings with influential community members. I took down the names of everyone who was involved or attended an event. Then on election day, I called on them to act as poll workers. We had an impressive list of dedicated volunteers.

I remember meeting at Marjorie's house in the cabana out back and that's where our first campaign offices were. It's where people like Jake Tapper started out working for her campaign. There were lots of interesting people coming and going, and it was quite exciting. Her children even got involved and would help every weekend when we went out campaigning and marching with signs. Everybody wanted to be a part of the momentum and excitement.

Arlene and many others were passionately dedicated to the effort to elect a woman, and that helped inspire me to push forward. Since I'd worked in journalism, I knew how the media operated and how important publicity was. My campaign generated a lot of attention and press coverage. Having produced many human-interest stories, I knew the angles were irresistible—first single person to adopt internationally, blended family, husband involved in politics, media personality—and that meant lots of attention for our campaign and our cause.

We chose to focus on three central themes: education, healthcare, and jobs. To win the historically Republican seat, we pointed out that I was a different kind of Democrat, a "small-d" democrat, one who wanted to not only examine the cost of social programs but also be fiscally responsible, a platform not typically associated with my party. Whenever I was asked, I'd say I was against raising across-the-board taxes. I knew I couldn't promise not to raise taxes, because there was no way to predict what issues we would face. However, the press reported that I'd said that I would *never* raise taxes. I didn't say that, but the truth was immaterial at that point. The "no tax increase" message was quickly imprinted on the minds of voters because that's what they were fed, and they wanted to believe it. No one *wants* higher taxes.

The constituents got to know me during the primaries, and apparently, we hit a chord because we won easily. The nonstop media attention certainly didn't hurt. Folks seemed to like the fact that while I was a political unknown, I'd been exposed to politics through my job and my marriage. It was a bonus that I was like a politician but without a voting record that could be used against me. In the democratic primary, I ran against Bernard Tomkin and won with 79% to his 21%. After that, the momentum increased dramatically, and we were full steam ahead.

Then, personal tragedy struck. In January of 1992, I drove up the driveway to see our beautiful home on fire! My heart sank as I watched the flames through the windows. It was rapidly gaining momentum, destroying everything in its path. It was determined that the culprit was the disastrous pairing of a space heater and a flowing curtain. Fortunately, none of us was injured, but the damage was extensive. Repairs were estimated to take over a year and we were forced to relocate.

Always optimistic, I was sure that construction would move swiftly so we moved everyone who was still living at home into a beautiful rental at the Pew Estates. However, true to form in the construction world, it took longer than planned, a full 18 months to be specific, before we could return to our home. It certainly changed the family dynamic. As Andrew remembers it, "Going through the fire brought the family together, but we all knew that afterwards we would likely have to scatter."

Despite all of that, we moved forward with the political campaign as the children eagerly pitched in, even wearing bright red t-shirts with "MMM for Congress" across the chest. In the general election, I faced off against Republican Montgomery County Commissioner Jon D. Fox, an ample man with an ill-fitting toupee. He was commonly referred to as "the prohibitive favorite." In that Republican district, the election was seen as just a formality to reach the inevitable conservative conclusion.

While we all remained optimistic, we were shocked when the polling showed that it would actually be a tight race. I couldn't believe it because I was sure that it would be a Republican landslide. My hope had been to at least make a presentable showing.

Just to make things more challenging, my daughter Lee Heh was planning her wedding at the same time. I hated that the campaign took so much of my time, but we all knew how important it was to at least make a valiant effort to get a decent turnout of supporters. Arlene was even kind enough to act as "wedding mother" to help Lee Heh with organizing her ceremony and sending out invitations. It was a crazy time. Let me just say, I don't recommend running a political campaign, surviving a fire, and planning a wedding at the same time...if you can avoid it!

It was important that our campaign message was presented in a way so that people understood that I was a different kind of candidate but not *too* different. The hope was to reassure the conservative base that while I brought plenty of typically liberal values, I certainly wasn't what would be considered "far left," and that was important. Being too far on either side of the political spectrum can alienate moderates and undecided voters long before they even hear the platform.

The messaging was to be clear and direct. I would be a proudly democratic candidate, but not necessarily a traditional one, "sane centered, moderate middle," small-d. While I wholeheartedly supported issues like pro-choice and gun control, I also felt that government spending should be thoughtful and controlled. To that end, I proposed that social programs should still be supported, but the costs could be better managed. That would avoid the two words that practically every voter despises, "tax increase."

With the mission in hand, my family on board, and an enthusiastic team of volunteers and supporters, we canvassed the hell out of our district. I knew it would be difficult, and it certainly was, but it was one of those synergistic moments where I was able to channel my energy, experience, and focus to achieve one goal: to win. And somehow, some way, that's exactly what happened. With over 250,000 votes cast, I won with 50.27% to my opponent's 49.73%, a difference of 1,373 votes.

When the result was announced, I was beyond surprised, and quite unprepared. I had only brought a concession speech to the watch party. (I'm nothing if not a realist.) And like anything I work toward, the satisfaction of not only meeting but crushing my goal, of beating the expectations, gave me that same shot of adrenaline I'd gotten in sports competitions or after landing a high-profile interview.

However, my real challenge, the part that I'm not so good at, is enjoying the success, whatever it may be. Many people would celebrate, revel in their victory, luxuriate in the satisfaction of it all. That has never been me. My focus is always on the next step. What do I have to do now? For me, it's not a time to sit back, but one where I need to look forward. I'm not sure if that's the healthiest approach, but it's all I know.

Only three days after winning the election, I was off to Washington. I knew it was early, but I was eager. Newly elected representative orientation was a month away. That would be followed by office assignments and then the swearing in ceremony. Having been on the periphery of the political realm, I knew how important it was to quickly secure an assignment on a committee that meant something to me, so I set my sights on the influential Energy and Commerce (E&C) Committee.

But first things first. I was sworn into office in a symbolic ceremony so that others could witness the event. Over 1,000 supporters and campaign workers took buses into Washington to attend the event. Ironically enough, I missed casting my first vote because of the required protocol. Fortunately, it was only a procedural one, but it still bothered me.

At the time, there was a congressman named William Natcher who had never missed a vote. He had cast over 18,401 of them in his career and one time they even brought him in on a stretcher to make his voice heard. When I told him how upset I was that I'd missed my very first vote, he said, "You are so lucky. It's too much of a responsibility to have never missed a vote."

With the E&C Committee in the forefront of my mind, I decided to contact Jack Murtha who was the head of my delegation. He was from Pittsburgh, the other side of the state, and since he was more conservative, I wasn't sure we'd have a lot in common. Some way, we struck up a friendship and he was incredibly kind to me. When it came down to it, despite our differences, we forged a lasting friendship. He even became my advisor, or maybe my confessor. I adored him.

The rest of the incoming representatives arrived in Washington on December 2nd. We were all going through an orientation process to learn about concepts like ethics and issues, not to mention committee assignments. However, it was different from previous years. Because of the hype over the large number of newly elected women, four of us were constantly followed by a camera crew as journalist Linda Ellerbee recorded our first 100 days in office for a documentary. I wore a microphone at all times and had to remember to remove it when I took a bio break.

I realized that being newly elected, I was low in the pecking order and prestigious assignments typically went to the more senior members. Yet, I remained steadfast. I was told by several higher-ups that women weren't typically on the E&C and that I didn't have the required legislative background.

At a group dinner, we were anxious to hear about our assignments. It was quickly announced that the female representative from Arkansas would get the E&C appointment. Since female members were rare, I figured that my odds had just decreased to practically zero. Then when I went to congratulate her on the assignment, a hand shot out in front of me. "Congratulations," said Mike Synar of Oklahoma, "you're on the E&C as well." Everything was falling into place.

I had a bit of a chuckle when Representative Barney Frank of Massachusetts welcomed me to Congress and said, "I want to congratulate you even if your campaign slogan missed the mark."

"What do you mean?" I asked.

"It should have been 'I'm going to pull the rug out from right on top of him!'" as he chuckled at his own joke about my opponent.

"A missed opportunity," I said with a smile.

Since my family was settled in Pennsylvania, I would commute back and forth by train as I had during my job at the news station. That way I could get plenty of work done on the train during the trip. Even back then, Joe Biden, a senator at the time, was known for being a proponent of the railway as he commuted to and from his Wilmington, Delaware home to Washington. I often ran into him on the train.

With the win, we immediately shifted into staffing mode. Fortunately, because we had such talented folks working on the campaign, many were able and willing to take a position in my Congressional office. Arlene accepted immediately and was a valuable member of the team. Because her husband was a doctor and she read everything related to medicine and politics, she was quite helpful with understanding the healthcare bill that Hillary Clinton was championing at the time. She also fielded calls from constituents and helped arrange meetings with other members of the House to discuss policy.

Many others joined as well, including Jake Tapper who had done an excellent job as my communications director during the campaign and then my press secretary. Of course, I'd known his parents for ages, even attending his bris! In fact, his dad, Ted Tapper, was our family doctor and all the kids called him "Uncle Ted." Sometimes they called him "Uncle Ten" because they thought he was so perfect. When I was just starting my career, I told him how I wanted to adopt. He said that if I ever adopted in the future, he'd take care of my kids' health as a courtesy. He had no idea what he was in for, but he fulfilled his promise with all my extended family.

Once fully staffed, it was exactly how I wanted the office to be: a place where people I could trust helped me tackle all the new information and the many challenges that were quickly thrust upon newly elected representatives. It was an overwhelming experience but one I wholeheartedly welcomed.

It was my goal to set a tone of collaboration and unity among the entire office because I'd been in so many situations where women were not only the minority but often practically invisible. This was my chance to run an office like one I'd want to work in. There would certainly be no tolerance for maligning anyone and all would be represented as long as they had something to bring to the table.

Fortunately, everyone responded as I'd hoped they would, and it not only felt natural but even fun if you can imagine such a thing in politics. We all genuinely enjoyed each other and felt passionate about our mission. Some of the key decisions I made during my tenure were:

- **Focusing on issues that would benefit women** such as abortion rights and access to quality healthcare. I strongly opposed the Hyde Amendment because it denied federal funding for abortions, and I supported breast and cervical cancer funding and research.

- **Voting for the Family and Medical Leave Act** which required employers to provide employees with unpaid leave for family/medical reasons with health coverage and job protection.

- **Supporting the Brady Handgun Bill** which required background checks and a waiting period before buying a gun.

I was quite proud of the fact that I was able to join the other representatives in providing a voice for women and effect change in an environment where men historically made those types of decisions for women. Not only that, but I was firm on my stance that none of these bills or proposed initiatives should result in a tax increase.

After about a year and a half in office, I was faced with the biggest challenge of my career. I'd prepared myself for making tough decisions and for the most part, I'd been able to navigate whatever came my way. In August of 1993, President Bill Clinton was seeking support for the Omnibus Budget Reconciliation Act that he had proposed in February of that year. It was also referred to as the Deficit Reduction Act of 1993.

When President Clinton won the election in 1992, the country was struggling to recover from a recession and the national debt had been a major issue of the election. To that end, he submitted a budget that would reduce the deficit by cutting spending and raising taxes. That was a non-starter for me. It was a contentious time in Washington and the country. To clarify my stance on the bill, I went on TV and reiterated my position. I was against the bill because I didn't think it made deep enough cuts and didn't address entitlements. I felt it important to keep my constituents informed of my thought process to clarify the "no tax increase" misinformation that was being reported.

President Clinton had asked those who were against the bill if he could count on their support, and I was clear that I would be a "no" vote. I still didn't think the bill went far enough with spending cuts. When I was on the House floor and votes were being cast, I was pulled aside. The President was on the phone. "What would it take to get your vote?" he asked.

Going into this, I knew there would be real challenges that I'd have to confront. I was determined to take each issue on its own merit and do what I thought was best for the country and specifically my constituents. We all knew that deal-making and concessions were part of the job. No one was going to be successful trying to bulldoze his or her way through the process. It would only serve to generate opposition and ill will. It was all about compromising and finding a middle ground where each side felt they were being heard.

Just as it had come back to haunt President George "Read My Lips" Bush, my strong initial stance on opposing an across-the-board tax increase may have been my demise because of the misunderstanding it caused. When I was campaigning, I felt strongly about it and hoped it would register with voters in my overwhelmingly Republican district.

The President said that since the bill had gone through so many machinations and was on the verge of passing, it was important that I did not oppose it just because of my one issue. In my heart I knew he was right. This would be a win for the party and the greater good, but there was one big problem. I would be the scapegoat. That was quite clear. So I informed him that I would vote yes only in the event of a tie. This was my one chance to negotiate so I told the President I would support the bill, but I needed something from him. He would come to one of the conferences scheduled in my district and explain to the public, my constituents, ways we could work to reduce the deficit and look at entitlement spending. That way, I felt the bill would pass, and I'd have the President himself answer to the folks in my district.

I knew it was a roll of the dice, but history was on my side. At that time, there had only been two instances of tied votes of this magnitude. One was the impeachment of Andrew Johnson in 1868 when the Senate came up with a tie vote, twice. The other was the vote on the peacetime draft in 1940 that narrowly passed with 203 to 202. What were the chances of that happening again? Those seemed like good odds to me.

Bill Clinton remembers it well:

> *When the voting began, I still didn't know whether we were going to win or lose. After David Minge, who represented a rural district in Minnesota, said he would vote no, it all came down to three people: Pat Williams of Montana, Ray Thornton of Arkansas, and Marjorie Margolies-Mezvinsky of*

Pennsylvania. I really didn't want Margolies-Mezvinsky to have to vote with us. She was one of the very few Democrats who represented a district with more constituents who'd get tax hikes than tax cuts. It was a tough vote for Pat Williams, too. Far more of his constituents would get tax cuts than tax increases, but Montana was a huge, sparsely populated state where people had to drive long distances, so the gas tax would hit them harder than most Americans. But Pat Williams was a good politician and a tough populist who deplored what trickle-down economics had done to his people. There was at least a chance that he could survive the vote.

Compared with Williams and Margolies-Mezvinsky, Thornton had an easy vote. He represented central Arkansas, where there were far more people who would get a tax cut than a tax increase. He was popular and could not have been blown out of his seat with a stick of dynamite. He was my congressman, and my presidency was on the line. And he had lots of cover: both Arkansas senators, David Pryor and Dale Bumpers, were strong supporters of the plan. But in the end Thornton said no. He had never voted for a gas tax before and he wouldn't start now, not to get the deficit down, not to revive the economy, not to save my presidency or the career of Marjorie Margolies-Mezvinsky.

Finally, Pat Williams and Margolies-Mezvinsky came down the aisle and voted yes, giving us a one-vote victory. The Democrats cheered their courage and the Republicans jeered. They were especially cruel to Margolies-Mezvinsky, waving and singing, "Good-bye, Margie." She had earned an honored place in history, with a vote she shouldn't have had to cast.

My thought process was that I was not there to be popular, but there to lead. Women had come to Washington to make real change. When the opportunity was put in front of me, when the

President promised that he would address entitlements, I had to put my trust in the process. Possibly to my detriment, I wasn't thinking about whether I'd win reelection or if the Democrats were happy with me and the Republicans angry. I had gone to Washington to make tough decisions and that was definitely one of the toughest.

As a side note, ultimately, according to www.factcheck.org the Clinton Administration was able to balance the federal budget and created a surplus of over $236.2 billion largely due to the tax increase that resulted from the 1993 bill passage, not to mention help lift the country out of a recession. In 1998, there was actually a surplus in the federal budget for the first time since the 1960s. Republicans had claimed that it was the largest tax increase ever, but that was simply not true. That title goes to Lyndon Johnson and his Revenue and Expenditure Control Act of 1968 which resulted in a 10% surcharge on income taxes for individuals and corporations. Once Congress adjourned, I sponsored a program on Entitlements at Bryn Mawr College in December of 1993 and President Bill Clinton attended as promised along with many cabinet members and financial experts.

Despite my efforts with the conference, the political fallout was swift and severe for Democrats as a whole and me specifically. I knew that I was falling on the sword for the greater good, but that didn't make it any easier during the melee that ensued. It started as I crossed the House floor to cast my vote. Bob Walker, a Republican from the other side of Pennsylvania actually began jumping up and down while chanting "Bye-bye, Margie!" First, I knew he was likely right, and second, I thought he was a very good jumper!

My vote pushed it over the edge and on to victory in the House. The bill would come to a tie in the Senate, straight down party lines, until Vice-President Al Gore broke it by casting the deciding vote with a final tally of 51-50.

Almost immediately, Arlene began fielding calls from Montgomery County residents who were upset, angry, and frustrated with me. The bill had been the topic of much discussion and debate for over seven months and the nation was transfixed. Everyone had an opinion, and after the vote, it was time for me to accept the consequences.

"We've had nonstop calls," Arlene said. It had started just as I cast the vote and showed no signs of subsiding. Republicans were vilifying me about "the vote heard around the nation." I was branded a liar, a "tax and *pretend* Democrat."

I did my best to right the tilting political ship by challenging Republican National Committee Chairman Haley Barbour to a debate after that committee ran inaccurate political ads leading up to our Entitlements Conference.

My "yes" vote was still fresh in voters' minds during my reelection campaign in 1994. Yet, we gave it our best shot despite the underlying reality that my vote had likely sidelined any future political ambitions. This time around, I was not the new candidate, and the PR angles of a blended family with adopted children were old news. There were few positive interviews and human-interest articles. The entire focus, the narrative pushed by the Republicans, was that I had lied and couldn't be trusted. Not to mention that I was blamed for raising taxes on the 1%, many of whom lived in my district.

There were a few glimpses of hope, an article that touted "Margolies-Mezvinsky to Defy Pundits' Crystal Balls" and another asking "Can Mezvinsky Score a Late Round Knockout?" with an illustration of me with boxing gloves, a bandaged nose, and stars swirling above my head. That was quite a change from the largely positive media reports from two years prior.

Republican groups came out in force against my campaign as their number one target and then they focused on other House Democrats who were also seeking reelection. It was a nonstop political onslaught, but it was not unexpected. I understood what I'd done and the potential consequences that would follow.

Traditionally, midterm elections signal the level of satisfaction with the sitting President who has two more years left in his term. The first brutal midterm attack on Democrats occurred in 1894 as Grover Cleveland was President and the country was dealing with a recession and rapidly growing unemployment numbers. One hundred years later, when all was said and done, the Democrats lost over 100 Congressional seats and the Republicans were in charge.

This time, Jon Fox, the same opponent I'd bested in 1992, won by 8,000 votes which came to 49% for him and 45% for me. To be honest, I did better than I had expected, but of course if you don't win, you've lost.

After the votes from the November elections were tallied, the political pendulum had swung to the right and Congress was under Republican control for the first time in over forty years. The 1994 election was even referred to as the Republican Revolution because at final count they had gained eight seats in the Senate and a whopping 54 in the House. This was partly accomplished by a strategy that featured the "Contract with America," proposed legislation that was written in part using language from one of Ronald Reagan's State of the Unions addresses. (We called it the Contract *On* America!) It was also the year of Newt Gingrich. Only two years prior, it had been the Year of the Woman. Politics is a fickle beast.

Once the democratic upheaval took place, all of those who had lost their seats were invited to the White House where we were consoled by Bill Clinton and Al Gore and thanked for our service. Many years later, in most of his speeches, Clinton said that he thought he raised taxes too much that year. Once he made that statement, I started to get calls from the media asking about my thoughts. "What is your reaction?" they wanted to know. I simply said, "Oh my." The next day, that two-word quote was on the front page of *The Wall Street Journal*.

Sometimes it helps to put things in perspective, but it still doesn't soften the blow. Being in a position to help people, especially women and children, was the perfect job for me. Having it taken away after only two years was tough. I'm a fighter, and I survived, but I still think about the difference I could have made had I been given the chance.

Since he was there, I asked my friend Joe Kennedy II to share his thoughts on that contentious period in U.S. politics.

I clearly remember the tension on Capitol Hill that steamy day in August as the debate over President Clinton's budget stretched long into the night. The vote on President Clinton's budget, which included a series of tax increases, finally came before the House after extensive deliberations. My friend Marjorie Margolies, the first Democrat elected in several generations from her suburban Philadelphia district, had spoken out against the budget but was under tremendous pressure from the leadership.

As she entered the chamber after nearly every vote was cast, Marjorie was surrounded by Members pleading their case. She told Speaker Foley that if she voted with Clinton, she would lose her district and that she would only vote yes if it came down to her holding the deciding vote. And that's exactly what happened. There was a tremendous sigh of relief from the budget supporters when she cast her ballot in favor of the budget. It was 218 to 216. Even a tie vote would have meant the defeat of the budget and perhaps the end of the Clinton presidency.

The fact is that Clinton had been pilloried for proposing a tax increase. While that horrible 'fact' is true, it is also true that passage of that tax hike put our country on one of the biggest comebacks in the history of the United States because it gave people a sense we were on our way to a balanced budget and fiscal responsibility. Predictions of an economic slump were proved wrong. The economy boomed, businesses prospered, job growth skyrocketed, and at the end of the Clinton presidency, a balanced budget was achieved, the national debt reduced, and a budget surplus handed over to his successor.

Marjorie's vote not only had huge positive consequences for our nation but was also the most courageous vote I've ever seen. People in America want leaders willing to vote for principles over politics. That's exactly what they got with Marjorie—someone who knowingly put her political career in jeopardy to do not what was easy but what was right. She stood up and did what Americans from all across the country, from every region and political party, want in their leaders— an authentic person showing personal and political courage.

I now teach a class at Penn along with David Eisenhower where we are able to debate topics such as political campaigns and conventions. We cover subjects ranging from the Charlottesville Unite the Right rally to Trump's impeachment and everything in between. We also touch on topics in the news like the children at the border, the proliferation of guns, and accessible healthcare.

Hopefully, my political experience can help educate and encourage future female candidates to run...and win.

CHAPTER 7

Under My Umbrella at the Fourth World Conference

There are some things you learn best in calm, and some in storm.

– WILLA CATHER, AMERICAN WRITER

COMPLETELY BY HAPPENSTANCE, I've been involved in a lot of situations throughout my life where I was either the only woman at the table or one of just a few. As I've mentioned, I was something of a first: the first single woman to adopt an international child, the first woman to win a Congressional seat in Pennsylvania in her own right, and when I became a journalist, I found out what it was like as a woman working in a male-dominated field.

I certainly didn't set out to accomplish those things for any reason other than the fact that I had been raised to believe I could do almost anything that I wanted to do. That assurance began with my parents. They taught me to stay true to my passions, and they supported my ambitions even if they thought I was a bit certifiable. Of course, they would have backed me up with the same fervor if I'd married right out of school and begun a family, but I think they always knew that wouldn't be the path for me.

The fact is, I wish I hadn't been in a position to be one of the few women at my workplace or the first to win a major office in the Keystone State, because that would have meant that there were many women before me. However, in the 1970s and 1980s, that just wasn't the case. Fortunately, our cultural landscape has changed in many ways.

I have always defined a family as a place where children can receive the love and support that they need to grow into healthy, productive, and happy adults. In truth, the look of families has been changing for years...thank goodness.

One-quarter to one-third of all families worldwide are headed by a single parent. In the United States, families rarely resemble the old stereotype of a nuclear family with a mother, father and 2.8 children. In fact, in almost half of all two-parent families in the US, both parents work outside the home (pre-COVID). It is difficult to have a conversation about families, much less address their needs in any meaningful way, unless we recognize and respect how the definition of a family has changed.

Clearly, the "typical family" has evolved extensively in the last 50 years, but social acceptance of alternative methods of building a family has not. When I was working at the NBC station in Washington, I had an amazing editor who was trying to start a family with her partner. Both of them were absolutely wonderful women, and I helped them navigate the adoption process so they could adopt a hard-to-place child. When I helped them inquire about the process, we were told that it would be better if she just said that she was single. It would be an easier path to adoption that way. I assisted another couple who adopted a child with a cleft palate.

Today, it's easier for *all* couples to adopt, but harder for anyone to adopt children from Korea. International adoptions can be cyclical, easier at times and then more difficult when laws change. The political landscape plays a large role in whether U.S. citizens are welcomed as potential parents.

Misunderstandings about the essential nature of families dogged the first Women's Rights Convention in Seneca Falls in 1848, "a convention to discuss the social, civil, and religious condition and rights of woman." About 200 women made great effort to attend, traveling long distances on horses and in carriages to make sure their voices were heard. At one point, the subject of women working outside the home came up. A gentleman farmer shared a thought held by many, "This will destroy the family." Despite the objections, the Declaration of Sentiments (or Declaration of Rights and Sentiments) was written primarily by a woman named Elizabeth Cady Stanton who modeled it after the Declaration of Independence. It was ultimately signed by 68 women and 32 men. By the time women were finally given the opportunity to vote in 1920, only one of the women in attendance at the convention was still alive to cast her vote.

More than 170 years later, the goal of the United Nations Fourth World Conference on Women came under similar attack. Some gave it the same label as that of the Seneca Falls Convention "an attempt to destroy the family." Those critics clearly did not fully understand the importance of the issues being discussed on a global scale. The World Conference on Women sought to enhance the lives of girls and women by improving access to health and education while condemning violence, abuse, and discrimination against women.

Anyone who has ever been faced with a family member's lump in her breast understands the agony felt by a husband or partner. Domestic violence is just as painful for a son to witness as for a daughter. The cost of education for girls worldwide will have the same benefits for male taxpayers as for female taxpayers. Girls and boys have an equal stake in their mother's economic security. These are family issues and must be recognized and treated as such. These issues matter, and they are not gender based. They impact everyone.

In 1995, I'd barely had enough time to dust myself off and get my bearings following my political freefall when I got a call from the White House asking if I'd lead the U.S. Delegation to the Fourth World Conference on Women held by the United Nations. I certainly couldn't turn down such an honor and historic opportunity, even though it was in the midst of controversy. The Republicans had taken control of Congress and didn't want to send a delegation to the conference and certainly didn't want First Lady Hillary Clinton to go.

The history of the World Conference on Women can be traced back to 1945 when the founding United Nations charter included a provision to promote gender equality, a forward-thinking initiative during the 1940s. Still, it wasn't until the late 1960s and early '70s that the women's movement began to gain some real traction. In 1975, the UN held the First World Conference on Women in conjunction with the International Women's Year. It took place in Mexico City and resulted in the adoption of a resolution titled "Declaration of Mexico on the Quality of Women and Their Contribution to Development and Peace."

The Second World Conference on Women occurred in 1980, this time in Copenhagen, with a focus on equal access to health care, education, and employment. Those three action items were a continuation of the conference in Mexico City. Five years later, the third world conference was held in Nairobi to examine the measured results of the advancements in women's equality. They were originally intended to take place every five years, but due to financial constraints, that duration was changed to every 10 years.

The Fourth World Conference on Women, with the subtitle

"Action for Equality, Development, and Peace," was convened on Monday, September 4, 1995, at the Beijing International Conference Centre. I was the head of the U.S. Delegation for the 10-day event with a total of 35,000 attendees and Hillary was the chair of our delegation. Prior to the trip, the delegation held many meetings at the UN to create the official document to outline our objectives. We had to be incredibly strategic with the language because we wanted to express our intentions and views but didn't want to alienate or create tension among the more conservative attendees, including China, our host country.

There were actually two conferences occurring simultaneously: the official one in Beijing and a separate event for the Non-Governmental Organizations (NGOs). The NGO conference was held in Huairou, about 30 miles north of Beijing. Theirs was "Look at the World Through Women's Eyes," and the meetings occurred in smaller groups on the campus of a run-down school. Each day, I made sure to take delegates from the official conference to the programs being held in Huairou. I felt it was important to hear their concerns on important topics like domestic violence, discrimination, and inequality.

Despite challenges like language barriers and cultural differences, we were able to diplomatically articulate our support of issues such as safe access to abortion for all women. Other topics, such as inheritance, that were seemingly benign in the U.S. were seen as quite controversial in countries like those in the Middle East.

One of the most remarkable moments of the entire convention was Hillary's speech. Initially, it was scheduled to be held outside to allow for a large number of attendees, but the weather had its own plans and that included lots of rain. The event was quickly moved to a theater, but it only held 1,500 people, not nearly enough.

Knowing that capacity was severely restricted, women began

arriving at 6:00 in the morning to get a seat. Soon, it was a logistical nightmare with thousands of women jockeying for a space as the rain bounced off the sea of primary-colored umbrellas. Some of the women from conservative countries even risked their own safety to witness the event.

It wasn't only our delegation that was under pressure to steer clear of controversy but Hillary's speech as well. She received word from the U.S. and our host nation of China to temper her message. Catholic groups were concerned that we were promoting a radical agenda. So, when she finally spoke, Hillary held true to her, and our, convictions to decry abuses against women around the world.

The speech is here in full, and I think it has the same impact it did when I heard it for the first time.

FIRST LADY HILLARY RODHAM CLINTON REMARKS FOR THE UNITED NATIONS FOURTH WORLD CONFERENCE ON WOMEN

BEIJING, CHINA
SEPTEMBER 5, 1995

Mrs. Mongella, Distinguished delegates and guests,

I would like to thank the Secretary General of the United Nations for inviting me to be part of the United Nations Fourth World Conference on Women. This is truly a celebration—a celebration of the contributions women make in every aspect of life: in the home, on the job, in their communities, as mothers, wives, sisters, daughters, learners, workers, citizens and leaders.

It is also a coming together, much the way women come together every day in every country.

We come together in fields and in factories. In village markets and supermarkets. In living rooms and board rooms.

Whether it is while playing with our children in the park, or washing clothes in a river, or taking a break at the office water cooler, we come together and talk about our aspirations and concerns. And time and again, our talk turns to our children and our families.

However different we may be, there is far more that unites us than divides us. We share a common future. And we are here to find common ground so that we may help bring new dignity and respect to women and girls all over the world—and in so doing, bring new strength and stability to families as well.

By gathering in Beijing, we are focusing world attention on issues that matter most in the lives of women and their families: access to education, health care, jobs, and credit, the chance to enjoy basic legal and human rights and participate fully in the political life of their countries.

There are some who question the reason for this conference. Let them listen to the voices of women in their homes, neighborhoods, and workplaces.

There are some who wonder whether the lives of women and girls matter to economic and political progress around the globe...let them look at the women gathered here and at Huairou...the homemakers, nurses, teachers, lawyers, policymakers, and women who run their own businesses.

It is conferences like this that compel governments and peoples everywhere to listen, look and face the world's most pressing problems.

Wasn't it after the women's conference in Nairobi ten years ago that the world focused for the first time on the crisis of domestic violence?

Earlier today, I participated in a World Health Organization forum, where government officials, NGOs, and individual citizens are working on ways to address the health problems of women and girls.

Tomorrow, I will attend a gathering of the United Nations Development Fund for Women. There, the discussion will focus on local—and highly successful—programs that give hard-working women access to credit so they can improve their own lives and the lives of their families.

What we are learning around the world is that, if women are healthy and educated, their families will flourish. If women are free from violence, their families will flourish. If women have a chance to work and earn as full and equal partners in society, their families will flourish.

And when families flourish, communities and nations will flourish.

That is why every woman, every man, every child, every family, and every nation on our planet has a stake in the discussion that takes place here.

Over the past 25 years, I have worked persistently on issues relating to women, children, and families. Over the past two-and-a-half years, I have had the opportunity to learn more about the challenges facing women in my own country and around the world.

I have met new mothers in Yogyakarta, Indonesia, who come together regularly in their village to discuss nutrition, family planning, and baby care.

I have met working parents in Denmark who talk about the comfort they feel in knowing that their children can be cared for in creative, safe, and nurturing after-school centers.

I have met women in South Africa who helped lead the struggle to end apartheid and are now helping build a new democracy.

I have met with the leading women of the Western Hemisphere who are working every day to promote literacy and better health care for the children of their countries.

I have met women in India and Bangladesh who are taking out small loans to buy milk cows, rickshaws, thread and other materials to create a livelihood for themselves and their families.

I have met doctors and nurses in Belarus and Ukraine who are trying to keep children alive in the aftermath of Chernobyl.

The great challenge of this conference is to give voice to women everywhere whose experiences go unnoticed, whose words go unheard.

Women comprise more than half the world's population. Women are 70 percent of the world's poor, and two-thirds of those who are not taught to read and write.

Women are the primary caretakers for most of the world's children and elderly. Yet much of the work we do is not valued—not by economists, not by historians, not by popular culture, not by government leaders.

At this very moment, as we sit here, women around the world are giving birth, raising children, cooking meals, washing clothes, cleaning houses, planting crops, working on assembly lines, running companies and running countries.

Women also are dying from diseases that should have been prevented or treated; they are watching their children succumb to malnutrition caused by poverty and economic deprivation; they are being denied the right to go to school by their own fathers and brothers; they are being forced into prostitution, and they are being barred from the ballot box and the bank lending office.

Those of us who have the opportunity to be here have the responsibility to speak for those who could not.

As an American, I want to speak up for women in my own country—women who are raising children on the minimum wage, women who can't afford health care or childcare, women whose lives are threatened by violence, including violence in their own homes.

I want to speak up for mothers who are fighting for good schools, safe neighborhoods, clean air and clean airwaves... for older women, some of them widows, who have raised their families and now find that their skills and life experiences are not valued in the workplace...for women who are working all night as nurses, hotel clerks, and fast food chefs so that they can be at home during the day with their kids...and for women everywhere who simply don't have time to do everything they are called upon to do each day.

Speaking to you today, I speak for them, just as each of us speaks for women around the world who are denied the chance to go to school, or see a doctor, or own property, or have a say about the direction of their lives, simply because they are women.

The truth is that most women around the world work both inside and outside the home, usually by necessity.

We need to understand that there is no formula for how women should lead their lives. That is why we must respect the choices that each woman makes for herself and her family. Every woman deserves the chance to realize her God-given potential.

We also must recognize that women will never gain full dignity until their human rights are respected and protected.

Our goals for this conference, to strengthen families and societies by empowering women to take greater control over their own destinies, cannot be fully achieved unless all governments, here and around the world, accept their responsibility to protect and promote internationally recognized human rights.

The international community has long acknowledged— and recently affirmed at Vienna—that both women and men are entitled to a range of protections and personal freedoms, from the right of personal security to the right to determine freely the number and spacing of the children they bear.

No one should be forced to remain silent for fear of religious or political persecution, arrest, abuse or torture.

Tragically, women are most often the ones whose human rights are violated. Even in the late 20th century, the rape of women continues to be used as an instrument of armed conflict. Women and children make up a large majority of the world's refugees. And when women are excluded from the political process, they become even more vulnerable to abuse.

I believe that, on the eve of a new millennium, it is time to break our silence. It is time for us to say here in Beijing, and the world to hear, that it is no longer acceptable to discuss women's rights as separate from human rights.

These abuses have continued because, for too long, the history of women has been a history of silence. Even today, there are those who are trying to silence our words.

The voices of this conference and of the women at Huairou must be heard loud and clear:

It is a violation of human rights when babies are denied food, or drowned, or suffocated, or their spines broken, simply because they are born girls.

It is a violation of human rights when women and girls are sold into the slavery of prostitution.

It is a violation of human rights when women are doused with gasoline, set on fire and burned to death because their marriage dowries are deemed too small.

It is a violation of human rights when individual women are raped in their own communities and when thousands of women are subjected to rape as a tactic or prize of war.

It is a violation of human rights when a leading cause of death worldwide among women ages 14 to 44 is the violence they are subjected to in their own homes.

It is a violation of human rights when young girls are brutalized by the painful and degrading practice of genital mutilation.

It is a violation of human rights when women are denied the right to plan their own families, and that includes being forced to have abortions or being sterilized against their will.

If there is one message that echoes forth from this conference, it is that human rights are women's rights...and women's rights are human rights.

Let us not forget that among those rights are the right to speak freely. And the right to be heard.

Women must enjoy the right to participate fully in the social and political lives of their countries if we want freedom and democracy to thrive and endure.

It is indefensible that many women in non-governmental organizations who wished to participate in this conference have not been able to attend, or have been prohibited from fully taking part.

Let me be clear. Freedom means the right of people to assemble, organize, and debate openly. It means respecting the views of those who may disagree with the views of their governments. It means not taking citizens away from their loved ones and jailing them, mistreating them, or denying them their freedom or dignity because of the peaceful expression of their ideas and opinions.

In my country, we recently celebrated the 75th anniversary of women's suffrage. It took 150 years after the signing of our Declaration of Independence for women to win the right to vote. It took 72 years of organized struggle on the part of many courageous women and men.

It was one of America's most divisive philosophical wars. But it was also a bloodless war. Suffrage was achieved without a shot fired.

We have also been reminded, in V-J Day observances last weekend, of the good that comes when men and women join together to combat the forces of tyranny and build a better world.

We have seen peace prevail in most places for a half century. We have avoided another world war.

But we have not solved older, deeply rooted problems that continue to diminish the potential of half the world's population.

Now it is time to act on behalf of women everywhere.

If we take bold steps to better the lives of women, we will be taking bold steps to better the lives of children and families, too. Families rely on mothers and wives for emotional support and care; families rely on women for labor in the home; and increasingly, families rely on women for income needed to raise healthy children and care for other relatives.

As long as discrimination and inequities remain so commonplace around the world, as long as girls and women are valued less, fed less, fed last, overworked, underpaid, not schooled and subjected to violence in and out of their homes, the potential of the human family to create a peaceful, prosperous world will not be realized.

Let this conference be our—and the world's—call to action.

And let us heed the call so that we can create a world in which every woman is treated with respect and dignity, every boy and girl is loved and cared for equally, and every family has the hope of a strong and stable future.

Thank you very much.

God's blessings on you, your work and all who will benefit from it.

Her famous words at the official formal conference echoed through the consciousness of women for decades to come.

The irony that Chinese women weren't even supposed to attend the speech of the convention that country was hosting was not lost on us. They attended at their own peril. We knew that the event would not be broadcast in the Chinese media, but that wouldn't stop it from traveling around the world. Those brave women who did manage to attend asked us for a printed copy of the speech because they feared it would be censored by their government, if it were reported at all.

At the Huairou conferences, one of the threads had been domestic violence, and it was quite controversial because of the cultural differences. In one of the presentations, a woman from central Africa stood up and said, "In my village, there was a woman who was abused every night. We could all hear her cries. It got so bad that we couldn't take it anymore. All of the women formed a circle around her hut and yelled to the man, 'Take one of us! Give her a break!' He never touched her again." Sometimes the direct approach is the most effective.

That conference in Beijing, China lasted from September 4-15 with over 17,000 "official" participants and more than 30,000 activists and other attendees. There were representatives from 189 governments, UN agencies, and other organizations around the world.

I had quite a bit of international experiences during my tenure as a news reporter, and I understood the plight of women, particularly in other areas of the world where advancement and equality were much slower than in the United States. The UN conference helped to amplify those issues that stuck with me.

After returning to the United States, the delegation was called to the White House to debrief and discuss the commitments that resulted from the conference. For me, it became clear that we needed to bring more women to the table. That's how the Women's Campaign International (WCI) organization was born.

CHAPTER 8

Women's Campaign International

"Human rights are women's rights...
and women's rights are human rights."

– HILLARY RODHAM CLINTON

WCI ENVISIONS A WORLD OF HOPE, courage, and compassion where equality and inclusion are at the core of all decision-making with values such as collaboration, empathy, transparency, and sustainability.

Our plan was to leverage the commitments that governments from around the world had made at the 1995 conference to uphold 12 areas of concern: poverty, education and training, health, violence against women, armed conflict, the economy, power and decision-making, institutional mechanisms for the advancement of women, human rights of women, the media, the environment, and the girl-child, a term that came from symbol languages to make the distinction between boys and girls.

Since WCI was founded in 1998, we have upheld that commitment through our work all over the globe and at home in Philadelphia, Pennsylvania. Being elected to office had given me an insight into how politics, funding, and organization work on a large scale, so my initial focus was on supporting women in public office. In WCI's inaugural program in Bosnia-Herzegovina in 1998, we worked with 200 political women leaders to increase women's political participation, resulting in 70 of the 200 women being elected to office. Within our training, WCI encouraged democratic approaches to resolve conflict and focused on implementing security-building measures in post-conflict Bosnia-Herzegovina.

In 1998, I met with Kathleen Hall Jameson, the head of the Annenberg School. It was her idea to provide a grant so that WCI could teach a course on empowering women in emerging democracies and even take students to some of the countries where WCI was doing work. The class was a success and the grant allowed us to travel to other countries. Our first trip was to Venezuela and then Uruguay. In 2001 it was Romania, which led to WCI training 150 women leaders, including city council members, politicians, and NGO leaders, in effective media advocacy and political leadership.

In 2003, throughout six major regions in Azerbaijan, WCI partnered with local women's organizations and trained more than 60 women leaders in political leadership, civic engagement, and voter mobilization, increasing the number of women in the National Assembly from 9.6% to 11.2%, and from 2002-2007, we expanded to Tanzania, Namibia, Ethiopia, Afghanistan, Azerbaijan, Malawi, and the Palestinian Territories. In 2003, we addressed social mobilization in Haiti.

In addition, since 2006, WCI has worked in Afghanistan with parliament and grassroots organizations educating and training women in leadership, communication, community mobilization, and entrepreneurship with the support of our Director of Programs in Afghanistan, Nasrin.

In the chaos that erupted during the withdrawal of US troops from Afghanistan in August of 2021, we spent many days working with the US government, our contacts in Kabul, to evacuate Nasrin. It was a truly harrowing experience, and although she endured many hardships, we did get her out. We also worked hard to get others out who worked with us.

After the US withdrawal, WCI received a letter from a noted professor and human rights activist in Kabul who we work with explaining the ongoing situation.

Since all civil society activists, such as human rights activists and women's rights activists, working in Afghanistan, are under the threat of terrorists and opponents of democracy, so the number of people who are threatened by terrorists is increasing day by day.

I have been working for many years for women to have access to their human rights in Afghan society. In fact, besides being professor, I have been member of various Civil Society Organizations, including Afghan Women Network (AWN). Meanwhile, I worked closely with the media as well.

At the beginning of the Peace Negotiation Process, I was a member of the Afghan Peace Negotiation Board as a representative of Civil Society, but after two months, I was removed for unknown reasons. Civil society organizations had a large scale of advocacy to have their representative in the Board but unfortunately it was unsuccessful.

Although I had threats before, after this case, some people came to me and asked me to participate as a member of the Taliban in the Peace Negotiation. Inasmuch as I did not accept their request, threats have been increased. Since I have young daughters and they are students and employed, they have been threatening me either to accept their request or they will harm my daughters or if I make this issue official, I cannot live for one more day.

During those days, my car was stopped by people who also had my photo with themselves and tried to attack me. Fortunately, I was saved by the cooperation of people.

During the Covid-19 pandemic in quarantine, I was safe from threats, but I still could not leave the house after the quarantine. A day I had a doctor's appointment. When I left there, on the way to home, a car, intentionally, crushed my car, but due to a traffic jam on the road which happened, the car escaped.

After the attack on Kabul University Campus on 2 November 2020 which targeted professors of Law and Political Science Faculty, my mental health is distressed and even it has become difficult for me to go out, I feel I will be attacked at any moment.

Recently, when the live classes started at university, I was in my office getting ready for a conference at which I was presenting a topic. A man entered my office who was looking like a student. He put his Samsung Galaxy phone on the table in front of me and told me to read the message. There was written: 'I am a representative of the Taliban. I want to talk to you for 10 minutes. Do not make any problem, otherwise it will not be good for you.' I asked him how he entered the university. He showed me his ID card, which was a student ID card with his name and department on it. He told me that he was there to ask me to join the group and work for them. He put three of my own written books, which are Women's Human Rights, Gender and Rights and Honor Killing, on the table and told me that they knew about all my Human Rights Activities. He also gave the addresses of my daughters, the one who is in school and the one who is a student at Kabul University. Since my Electronic ID (Tazkire Electronic) process had some administrative problems, he told me that 'on this date your daughters have taken their electronic IDs, why have you not?'. He also gave my husband's details which he is retired and was working as a legal advisor for the Human Rights Commission in Kabul.

When I got to know that he had all my information, I asked him what he wanted from me. He told me that as being Muslim, I must work with them. But my response was that I am only a human rights activist, and I am happy about that. Before leaving the office, he said that he was going to be back, and I had to think about what he talked about. After that, he, again, put his phone in front of me and wrote: 'If you complain about this conversation or talk about this to anyone in the university, not just you, also your daughters will be killed.'

The last practical threat I faced at the end of June was in front of the northern gate of Kabul University, which frightened me even more. One day, as I was crossing the road in front of Kabul University's north gate, a white Corolla car turned around and shouted at me to stop and pointed a gun at me, while the police in front of the university gate rushed to my aid. When the driver noticed the police, he turned the car off the road and escaped.

All these threats and bad situations have been taking me away from professional life and all human rights activities, but now even leaving home for doctor appointments will risk my life.

Since Taliban took over, I left my primary home, with my family and I am staying with one of my married daughters close to Kabul airport. Taliban has started door to door searches, and I am living with the fear that they might find me and kill me and take my daughters with them. We have decided that if they found us, we are going to jump out of the window and kill ourselves because I cannot even imagine what Taliban would do to me and my daughters.

As of this writing, we have been unable to get her, her family, and any others out of the country. They are still in hiding. We also worked with two government ministers who were known for being supportive of women's rights. One was killed by the Taliban, and we were able to get the other one safely to Pakistan along with his family.

From 2002-2007, WCI has worked with local partners in Malawi to train women in political participation, HIV/AIDS awareness, and legal advocacy. Of the 155 women who ran for office, over half of the candidates attended WCI's workshops. In addition, in 2021, WCI brought our Reducing Adolescent Pregnancy (RAP) in the Era of COVID-19 program to Malawi.

For me, one of the outcomes I'm most excited about was that after we went into Malawi for the first time, the number of women in parliament doubled. In fact, early in one of our programs came a woman named Callista Chimombo, an amazing and dynamic person.

Callista is known as being unapologetically vocal about her political views and has an impressive number of accomplishments under her belt. She was a member of the Malawi Cabinet as the National Coordinator of Maternal, Infant, and Child Health and HIV/Nutrition/Malaria and Tuberculosis. On top of that, she's active in charity work promoting safe motherhood. While WCI certainly can't claim responsibility for all her success, she is a shining example of what we hope our program members are able to achieve.

In Malawi, Callista has built an impressive career. She was Secretary of the Malawi Women's Caucus, a member of the pan-African Parliament, and Minister of Tourism and Culture in Malawi. Later, she was asked to join President Bingu wa Mutharka's Cabinet. She ended up marrying him and becoming an actual First Lady of Malawi, which led to WCI's First Ladies Initiative. Callista says, "After WCI began running workshops for aspiring MPs, the number of women in parliament doubled. A truly groundbreaking achievement that changed the political landscape of Malawi so deeply and profoundly that in 2012 Malawi enjoyed its first female president."

The First Ladies Initiative involved 18 countries including Cameroon, Benin, Gabon, Mozambique, The Gambia, and Guinea Bissau. This commitment involved developing and defining the role of the African First Lady and providing a platform for current and future First Ladies to use their unique political positions and passions to enact positive social change within their countries. That was made possible through the generosity and support of Judith Rodin and the Rockefeller Foundation. A caveat was that we had to be careful that the issues we dealt with were humanitarian, not political.

In order to empower these women, numerous challenges and organizational issues had to first be overcome. WCI began by identifying interested and committed First Ladies and then conducted assessments for each country. Those assessments helped gauge the current infrastructure within the Office of the First Lady, including the experience level of the staff and the availability of resources.

In 2011, WCI conducted a weeklong training for the First Ladies concurrent with the African Union summit in Ethiopia. These training workshops allowed each First Lady to decide on a relevant Legacy Campaign and provided dynamic networking opportunities between the women. The training culminated with individual sessions aimed at offering technical support to each of the First Ladies on her "Legacy Campaign." During these sessions, WCI staff provided each First Lady with a mentor to support her and her campaign efforts throughout the year.

WCI conducted 12 bilateral meetings and four in-depth consultations with First Ladies, their representatives and/or their advisors at the African Union Summit in Addis-Ababa, an interactive workshop with 17 African Ambassador's wives who would then share information with their respective First Ladies, deliver a comprehensive curriculum and resource package (both in French and English) to 27 Offices of the First Lady, and offer a series of interactive Skype sessions to First Ladies' technical advisors.

Beginning in 2007, partnering with local grassroots organizations in Colombia, WCI trained more than 300 women representing numerous regional women's networks in leadership advocacy, and institutional strengthening. We facilitated a program focused on human rights law for 230 women and led a workshop for both women and men centered on communities' spiritual traditions and achieving gender equality.

Another successful initiative that started in 2007 is the WCI work in Liberia. Our work in Liberia started following a conversation I had with Congressman Jack Murtha, in which I told him, "You know, women do not have a seat at the peace negotiation table in many economically challenged countries. WCI is making a difference and can continue to do so with support." He agreed and was able to help us obtain a $1.8 million grant. With that, we went into Liberia and took a multi-stakeholder approach—working with grassroots organizations, Goldman Sachs' 10,000 Women Initiative, and UNICEF—to train women in conflict transformation, political participation, and entrepreneurship.

A woman named Pam White, the head of USAID mission, was already doing important groundwork there and was quite supportive of our efforts. We went into every single village with local trainers who helped women by providing information like financial literacy and healthcare. When an Ebola outbreak hit that nation, the women were more equipped to help their communities navigate that challenge. It's a disease of information. They learned about the disease and how to inform the community to combat it effectively.

When we were in Liberia, USAID Mission gave us a series of grants that allowed us to work there for many, many years. Through this partnership, we trained and empowered thousands of women to strengthen their communication skills. A lot of it was making sure they understood how much more effective they would be if they formed collectives. When Ebola struck, essential to stopping the spread of the disease was information, and our women were able to handle this based on their training in effective communication provided by WCI. The women's networks in Liberia were largely credited with stopping the spread of the disease. It was amazing.

Susan Cox joined our board and has been involved for over 15 years, eventually become head of the board. As an adoptee and with her experience working with USAID through Holt, she provides an important perspective as the organization has changed with the times. "During a crisis like Ebola, it was important to have people on the ground. That's what WCI does so well. Going into another country to bring about change has to be at the grassroots level. They must believe in the cause, and WCI helps to facilitate that. That involvement at the local level encourages involvement of high-level officials who want to be connected with something that's seen as positive and important. That's always been a component of how WCI works out in the world."

WCI's largest initiative was implemented with the State Department and USAID in the MENA region (Middle East Northern Africa) across 16 different countries. WCI recognized women's full inclusion and participation in society was and still is vital for countries to develop into democratic, transparent, and economically prosperous nations. At a time when the level and nature of efforts toward women's empowerment vary tremendously across the region, effective collective and regional mobilization is essential to protect, consolidate, and advance the region's movement toward greater gender equality.

To foster such collective regional efforts toward the advancement of women's full leadership and participation in society, ALWANE was formed. ALWANE stands for Active Leaders for Women's Advancement in the Near East. In Arabic, "alwane" (pronounced Al-WA-nee) means "my colors," a phrase which evokes both the ability to paint our own future and the power of diversity in leading change.

More than 320 men and women academics, activists, experts, entrepreneurs, and youth from across these 16 MENA countries committed to social change and gender equality. Working at both a national and regional level, ALWANE aimed to generate discourse around pressing challenges to women's full participation in society, sharing intra-regional success stories, and creating fundamental change through targeted and wide-reaching advocacy and policy work surrounding women's rights and participation in society.

In just one year, the coalition's use of innovative technologies, engagement of young, new voices, and unprecedented intra-regional collaboration has resulted in inspiring stories of nation-wide advocacy and awareness efforts, and policy work that can motivate lasting change across the MENA region.

After more than a decade of working with women and girls all over the world, we realized it was time to bring our programs home to support girls in Pennsylvania. For years, many people in West Philadelphia had shared with me the need for a program for girls in Philadelphia. In 2010, WCI's Girls Advocacy and Leadership Series (GALS) was created as a weekly program run from WCI's office. Every Saturday morning, the participants would gather to learn advocacy and leadership skills and create real world change in their communities.

The GALS program has since expanded into an in-person after-school program where girl-identifying teenagers ages 13-17 gather twice a week to learn leadership skills and work on advocacy campaigns that they implement in their communities. The program is currently facilitated at First Philadelphia Preparatory Charter School and Bodine High School for International Affairs, and WCI is set to expand the program to reach students in many more schools across Philadelphia and Montgomery County. In addition, in 2019, WCI brought the GALS program abroad to Kenya.

Sofia Tamimi, WCI's Program Director, currently oversees the GALS program. She shares, "The goal of GALS is to empower disenfranchised teens and provide them with the skills and support they need to become leaders in their communities." The traditional GALS program is 18 weeks long and touches on topics including personal power, mindfulness, conflict management, strong women in history, self-esteem and self-worth, effective communication, healthy relationships, sexual and reproductive health, career and college planning, budgeting, resume writing, and even interview practice.

In addition to these workshops, the participants create and implement advocacy campaigns. Sofia shares, "It's exciting to support the girls while they select an issue that's important to them, something they're passionate about, and walk them through exploring the causes and consequences of that issue, setting a goal for their campaign, and actually implementing the campaign in their communities. Some of the topics that they've worked on in the past are LGBTQ+ rights, gender equality, deportation, animal abuse, educational justice, and mental health."

During the COVID-19 pandemic, WCI acted quickly to adjust our GALS program to a virtual platform. In the fall of 2020, WCI successfully piloted our first virtual eight-week GALS series with an incredible lineup of women speakers, including GALS alumni, facilitating workshops on topics from college planning and resilience to yoga and photography.

The success of this eight-week pilot program led us to create our second edition of the virtual GALS program, GALS: Game-changers, where we were able to bring in an array of women guest speakers who work in historically male-dominated fields to speak to the GALS participants about how they got into their field and the day-to-day work they do now. Speakers have included the Hon. Annette Rizzo (Ret.); a tech entrepreneur, Marti Griminck, founder of International Connector; a software engineer; two veterinarians who were graduates of UPenn's veterinary school; and artists who use their work to highlight social justice issues among many others.

Sofia says, "It's inspiring seeing the participants grow into confident young women who are incredibly supportive of each other. We constantly receive feedback from the girls asking if we can extend the program because they don't want it to end, and we consistently find participants who joined us as freshmen come back year after year." Sofia especially loves hearing the girls share feedback about their interactions with each other.

Sofia has done a great job of managing that program during a challenging time. For me, some of the touchstones of true success of an organization like WCI are attracting such passionate team members and being able to make our programs adaptable. We made GALS a viable virtual platform, and most recently we've leveraged our participants' standing in their communities to help with education about COVID-19 to include safety precautions and the truth about vaccines.

In order to assess the success of our programs, WCI implements proven monitoring and evaluation methods, including a primary and secondary evidence-based evaluation effort using a participatory mixed methods approach. The main objective is always to assess the outcomes of the program, with reference to how the program operated, whether or not it achieved its goals, and how it can be improved, sustained, and scaled along with allowing WCI to learn about the program's strengths and weaknesses. To achieve this, we conduct participant and trainer interviews, review secondary data, and analyze qualitative observational data. Through the use of these methods, we have compiled data that shows the program supports and improves key leadership skill competencies and has been effective in doing so by building an inclusive environment for learning and enacting social change.

In addition, the outcomes and impact of the GALS program show that the participants are also gaining firsthand experience designing and implementing community-based advocacy efforts to create change. The areas of growth include: Empathy, Self-Confidence, Career Goal Setting, Decision-Making, Self-Efficacy, Problem Solving, Local Awareness, Willingness to Learn, and Communication Skills.

The outcomes of the data suggest that increased growth in empathy, self-confidence, and goal setting have been some of the most significant changes among the participants. The program has been successful in implementing and promoting an inclusive learning environment for young teenage girls through a trauma-informed approach, contribution of dedicated staff, and pragmatic curriculum that meets the needs of the GALS participants. GALS sessions have positively created a process for girls to develop and implement action plans to support their efforts in community-level advocacy through weekly advocacy campaign group work.

That has been my goal for WCI from the very beginning: building up women, providing them with opportunities they may not have had, and helping them become responsible citizens of their community. Of course, along with this type of work comes many challenges.

Securing funding is my primary focus because without it, we can't make the difference in these young girls' lives. Our mission is to expand funding to sustain and strengthen the collaboration with community and local learning opportunities and resources for the participants as well as for the organization. We also want to host and facilitate more youth leadership and girl-empowerment-focused training for coaches to deliver leadership sessions that address the girls' needs and help improve their leadership development.

Another program that we're particularly proud of is our *RAP in the era of COVID-19*, which we rolled out in Kisumu, Kenya, during the global pandemic. In fact, we had accepted Mandela fellows during a summer exchange program, and the RAP program developed during that fellowship.

When COVID-19 brought international travel to a standstill in March of 2020, our staff had their bags packed to head to Kenya to facilitate our second GALS program. Since this was no longer possible, WCI worked with our partner, Prescilla Awino, founder of Winam Green Ventures (WGV), a women-led local community organization based in Dunga Beach- Kisumu, to create a program that fit the current needs of the girls in Kenya.

Prescilla shared with us that due to COVID-19 pandemic, the girls were not able to attend school. This increase in their free time led to an increase in the number of teenagers who were getting pregnant. With this information, WCI adjusted our GALS curriculum and RAP was born.

RAP originated as a four-week pilot program funded by a member of WCI's Board, Edie Hunt, that engaged 15 adolescent girls per week in socially distant gatherings. The workshops provided participants with critical resources, support, and information to prevent them from becoming pregnant, acquiring HIV, and spreading COVID-19. The RAP initiative was directly tied to the model and goals of WCI, building off past work that focused on health messaging and youth development.

In addition, WCI took into consideration the economic stress that COVID-19 has caused for many families; WCI understood that not every participant had sufficient food or personal items at home, and that when girls are menstruating without proper products or are hungry, they are less likely to attend gatherings and be active participants. To address these needs, each participant was provided with a resource package including PPE, underwear, toilet paper, pads, condoms, lotion, and food.

The pilot program was successful in implementing and promoting an inclusive learning environment through a trauma-informed facilitator and a culturally relevant curriculum that met the needs of RAP participants. The program outcomes demonstrated that participants gained knowledge on how to practice healthy habits in their relationships and personal lives and became part of a supportive, women-led community.

Based on the success of the pilot program in Kenya, WCI partnered with Ukani Malawi co-founders, Temwa Chirembo and Modester Mangilani, to facilitate a six-week RAP initiative with three weeks of the program being facilitated outside the city of Blantyre and three weeks in the rural town of Balaka. Six-week-long cohorts of 15 girls were trained, engaging a total of 90 participants over the course of the project. Each cohort attended workshops that discussed the basics of COVID-19, the female reproductive system and menstruation, consent and healthy relationships, preventing pregnancy and sexually transmitted diseases, and mental health.

Brynn MacDougall, WCI's former Director of Programs and Operations, and Temwa Chirembo received a grant from the Citizen Diplomacy Action Fund to implement this rendition of the RAP program. The Citizen Diplomacy Action Fund is sponsored by the State Department's Bureau of Educational and Cultural Affairs and implemented in partnership with the Partners of the Americas. The fund provides small grants to teams of U.S. citizen alumni of U.S. government-sponsored exchange programs to carry out public service projects that address the themes of media literacy education, building community resilience, and fostering alumni network development.

As an alum of the Mandela Washington Fellowship Reciprocal Exchange, Brynn applied for the grant with Temwa Chirembo, an alumnus of the Mandela Washington Fellowship, and became one of 38 successful applicant teams.

While the RAP program was being facilitated in Kenya and Malawi, many participants and parents of participants came to our trainers to ask if their friends, daughters, and younger siblings could participate in the sessions. Due to safety concerns and social distancing requirements, WCI was only able to host 15 participants per week, but in the future, pending viable funding, we are hopeful we will be able to bring the RAP program back to these interested women and girls along with expanding to other areas where this information and training is so greatly needed.

As with all of WCI's programming, we engaged in an evaluation to assess the outcomes of the RAP programs, with reference to how the program operated, whether or not it achieved its goals, and to generate key lessons and identify best or promising practices for learning, in addition to areas for improvement. Similar to the GALS evaluations, WCI used a primary and secondary evidence-based evaluation effort, using a participatory and mixed methods approach to assess the effectiveness and the scalability of the RAP pilot program. To gather valid and reliable data, we collected participant surveys, engaged in participant interviews, and monitored progress through weekly team discussions.

One of the most striking things that I learned from the facilitation of the RAP program pertains to the concept of consent. I was shocked to learn that at the start of the program, most participants did not know the meaning of consent, but you don't have to take it from me; one participant from the RAP Malawi program reported: "I learned to say no when I don't want to do something and the importance of agreeing to what both parties are comfortable with in a relationship," while another said, "I really liked the session on consent, this was a new term to me and I am glad I can now confidently set personal boundaries and say no or call people out when they violate these boundaries." Assistant Trainer Jennifer noted: "The girls were happy to learn about the female reproductive system and expressed that they haven't had this conversation in a safe space like this.... Many of them said they had not heard of the word consent or considered that they have a right to be in healthy relationships and only engage in activities they fully want to."

While our work started with a focus on increasing women's political participation and engaging in social mobilization campaigns to increase women's leadership, soon the programs began to reflect two other needs identified by the women we worked with: economic empowerment and conflict mitigation. Today, our initiatives focus on three main program themes: community engagement, economic sustainability, and conflict transformation. Our commitment to innovation and evidence-based decision-making has allowed us to easily adapt to meet the ever-evolving needs of women and girls, both locally and globally.

From building a youth leadership pipeline in Philadelphia and training businesswomen in the Middle East, to engaging in conflict transformation facilitation in Southeast Asia and skill-building with women politicians in Africa, we have worked passionately for more than two decades to empower women to transform their communities.

As you can tell, I'm quite proud and passionate about what WCI stands for and the sheer number of women around the world who have been empowered as a result of our efforts. It's my hope that other women, future generations, will not have to deal with being a "first" because it is no longer a rarity to have female representation and leadership in all facets of society.

I don't think I would have had the drive and commitment to create an organization like WCI without the unwavering support my parents provided. That solid foundation and willingness to go along with all my unconventional ideas helped convince me that I should do what I could to help level the playing field for women.

To me, it's clear that women are the center of all communities, and our voices are powerful. Currently, women make up about 49.6% of the world population but only 38% of the "formal" workforce. Economic inclusion of women creates opportunity for upward mobility in sectors such as education, business, and finance. That, in turn, creates expertise, income, and financial growth that would have otherwise not existed if women relied solely on a partner or family's income.

I faced many challenges in my career because it was a different time. Fortunately, I was not averse to taking risks in my work and personal life. Sometimes that strategy worked and sometimes it failed miserably, but that's how I learned. It's my hope that through the work of groups like Women's Campaign International, women are provided with helpful information, inspiring role models, and limitless opportunity.

One of my goals as a mother has been to show my children, especially my daughters, that it's important for women to not only speak up but to have our voices heard. Hopefully, I've demonstrated that goal through my personal and professional choices. Obviously, I haven't been afraid to fail; that has served me well, because I've clearly made missteps.

Taking chances has been a part of my journey for as long as I can remember. Hopefully, future generations of women won't have to confront many of the same challenges my generation encountered. I would be honored to be remembered for making even a small contribution toward helping women get a seat at the table.

I know my parents would be proud.

CHAPTER 9

The Art of Resilience

What happens is not as important as how you react to what happens.

– ELLEN GLASGOW, AMERICAN NOVELIST

IN THE LATE 1990S, Holly moved to Idaho and made a life for herself there, and she wrote about her relocation.

> *I realized a long time ago that it wasn't the world but me, that I choose to interpret my surroundings as a hostile place. Consequently, I don't ever let people know how easily I bruise. That's because most of the time, they cannot win. Meaning, no matter what others do or don't do, I am always negatively affected. Alas, once I realized this was my issue, I stopped blaming people or viewing myself as a victim of a cruel world. Instead, I recognized the defect and focused on damage control. For example, I compensate for my chronic fear of rejection by not going out much. I also prefer to eat in the women's room when forced to dine in public.*
>
> *I think one's natural reaction is to fix when experiencing something broken. I know I did. For example, I spent years*

of time and tons of money on therapy, medication, self-help books, yoga, and energy bars in an effort to improve myself, be happier. Short term, these activities definitely distracted my attention. But that's all they really were, distractions. By and by, I found myself constantly spinning around the 'improve yourself' idiot wheel, exhausted and broke. Finally, I woke up one day and said, 'fuck it.' I'm going to accept me and ride the consequence. I moved to Idaho.

Life in Idaho is categorically better. It just seems to flow, albeit clogged in one area while cascading in another, but it flows. Sentiments of being stuck or feeling like a hybrid between Spam and Scrapple cease to dominate my thoughts. In brief, I think I finally like me, I'm content. But this didn't happen overnight! God no! So many lessons were learned and re-learned before reaching this calm plateau.

In the process of buying a condo, she met an attorney named Doug. I can remember her calling me one day and saying, "Mom, are you supposed to get married or pregnant first?"

"Is he a member of the same species?" I asked.

When they married, I became the proudest of mothers. They had two sons, Jude and Trent, and I think that what had happened in her childhood made her own family all the more special and important to her.

I was making some changes of my own, and not all of them were anticipated. Just as WCI was ramping up, I experienced extreme personal loss much more devastating than any political defeat. My beloved mother Mildred passed away on May 4, 2000. (My father, "Pop-pop," had passed in 1986.) She was a staple in the area with many friends and family. Her memorial was a huge local event with much of the family contributing to the service. Holly spoke at the memorial with her trademark aplomb. People still talk about it to this day.

Funerals suck—especially if it's someone you know.

*But this one is a little more tolerable because it belongs to a life that was rich with experience that most of us will never be privy to. Look around you now and you will see the faces of friends and family who all called Mildred, Nanny. You see among you the first wave—Marjorie, Phylis, and Vicky. Among these daughters sit **their** children: Lee Heh, et al and Alan, etc. and Susan yadda yadda. Finally, the most recent additions are the great grandchildren: anything under six in this room mostly likely satisfies this category. And the most miraculous attribute of all these lives is that Mildred directly affected all, indeed caused their very existence.*

I refrain from crying because that communicates a want of sadness, and at this moment, I am very proud to have met such an extraordinary creature as my grandmother. Her company will undoubtedly be missed, but it's her character that I will most remember.

I would like to share with you now one of my fondest memories of Nanny. It was the last time I saw my grandmother, and I am grateful it was filled with laughter, smiles, and warmth.

My mother and I went to see my grandmother with the particular purpose of filling her balcony with flowers. Since her favorites were not on sale, we managed to capture ones that, while not the prettiest, were alive. While she sat on her terrace like a well-established southern woman, Mom and I dug and sowed her emerging garden. Conversation was light, mainly kept to the weather and how these plants were truly ugly. Our chatter was punctuated by updates of lives near and far, some of the gossip was true, others were, well, let's say were for purely entertainment purposes. But the weather was fine—sun shining and wind mild—so the gardening continued.

Finally, we were done with the city garden, but it still lacked something undefined but highly noticeable. It was then that I glanced to the corner of the balcony and noticed a statuette, a figure of Mother Mary with child; it was pink and very shiny. My first thought was "that thing will do quite well among these flowers, it is equally ugly." So, without hesitation, I grabbed the statuette and placed it dead center of our flower display. Ladies and gentlemen, we had ourselves at that very moment an official manger...the best Jewish manger I've ever witnessed.

As the three of us stood back and took the scene in, there was silence. Nanny was the first to break the silence, and with such eloquence. I fear I will not do it justice in my recall, but her words I will never forget....

"WHAT THE HELL IS THAT?"

With these words, all three of us nearly fell off the balcony in tears of laughter. While my mother had a hard time breathing through her tears, I had to sit down to stop mother nature from ruining my pants. After several minutes of the aforementioned, we recollected ourselves and began to strategize. The first order of business, to dismantle the manger. The second order of business, to cover the garden with a sheet. Finally, the last order of business, return to the apartment and eat lunch.

Lunch was eaten and the visit ended with hugs and kisses. Because of my home so far away, I instinctively knew this was the last time I would see my grandmother alive. There was a pause in my embrace. I hugged her longer than usual and when we said goodbye, I felt the tightness of my heart. My mother and I walked to the elevator in silence.

It was, indeed, the last time I saw my grandmother.

Nanny, much love. I will remember you.

Holly

That year yielded yet another loss. By that time, Ed and I were traveling separately. He'd never been a good traveler, but something had changed. In fact, his anger became increasingly more difficult for me to handle. At first, I brushed it off as a quirk, one of his few weaknesses, his Achilles heel. Over the years the seemingly irrational fears and unprovoked irritation increased in frequency and intensity regardless of the mode of travel.

In the car, he would grip the steering wheel as if it were coated with oil, like it was going to slip away at any moment. He was quick to get upset and complain about the other drivers, angered in a way that I rarely saw in any other situation. The airport experience was no different, and I could never pinpoint the cause. Still the questions remained. Where did this behavior originate? What was going on? Should I be concerned? What could I do?

Looking back, I did sense the increased tension, but it was so gradual that I never spoke of it. I tried to see if others felt the same, but when people came over, they seemed indifferent, as if nothing had changed. He would frequently travel alone, often out of the country, for business. When he was home, he used his office more and the rest of the house less. He would shut the door, and we all knew to leave him alone, and we did. Something seemed off, but I didn't know what it was.

Later, Holly told me that sometimes she'd hear him up late at night, his office door would slowly creak open, and she'd hear his determined footsteps up and down the hall as he paced back and forth. Maybe I should have been more in tune to what was happening at home, but I was in the middle of a U.S. Senate campaign and had little time for much else.

Finally, I found the source of some of the tension when he ran into some serious legal issues that took me completely by surprise. Later, he was diagnosed as bipolar, and it helped explain some of the behavior that had concerned me.

It was devastating for me and the rest of our family because we had no idea what had taken place. I had to come to terms with the fact that as an educated, progressive, independent woman, I had allowed my husband to handle all the finances because it didn't interest me. That wasn't my strong suit, and I trusted him completely to do what was best for our family. It seemed normal to me because my father had filled the same role in our home when I was growing up. I finally made the incredibly painful decision to file for divorce, and our family was never the same after that.

One surreal event was when Holly was living in Idaho and wanted to come home for a "surprise" wedding. She asked if I could help plan an event where she would announce her engagement to everyone, only the twist was that a wedding would actually take place! It was a very Holly move. I was able to pull together a perfectly lovely affair, and the event went along smoothly. The only distraction? Having Ed (the "wasband") attend the ceremony on his last day of freedom before he was to report to prison. Lives were crossing paths in that room, one whose marriage journey was just beginning as another's freedom was coming to an end. Only Holly's dynamic personality could have competed with such a formidable distraction.

It was the most challenging time of my life. I'm not sure how I got through that period, and if I'm honest, I'll never truly recover from it. But as Susan Cox says, "Marjorie's not just a glass half-full person. She's a glass half-full with a pitcher on the way."

I'm not completely convinced of that, but I like to think she's right. I would add that I was born on a sunny day, and that must account for something.

CHAPTER 10

A Force of Nature

I think one of the perks of passing away is that all those crappy gifts given to friends over the years are now their most sacred possessions. There is comfort in that for the deceased; memorialized in a horrid polyester lime-green scarf for eternity.

– HOLLY MARGOLIES WERTH

WHEN HOLLY WAS OUT ON HER OWN, our relationship evolved into a mother-daughter friendship, and we spent a lot of time together enjoying each other's company. One of the most special times was when we went back to visit Vietnam when she was 43, which was 37 years after her adoption. She had never wanted to return before that, but for some reason she was finally ready.

I was on a Presidential Commission called the Vietnam Education Foundation (VEF), a fellowship program with a mandate to enhance relations between the U.S. and Vietnam through international education exchange programs. I was there to interview young scientists who wanted to become part of the program. Holly asked if she could come along. I approached the commission and made the request to see if she could join the program and go to Vietnam, which they agreed to.

Susan Cox helped with locating some of Holly's family so we could meet them once we arrived. It was a huge adventure for both of us. Our family had been helping Holly's biological family for a long time by sending a couple hundred dollars a month to the agency. The money gave them the ability to find better accommodations, and they didn't have to beg in the streets anymore.

The family was excited to finally see Holly. Really excited. We sat around for a long time talking through a translator. They even located Holly's childhood babysitter and brought her to visit. The family hadn't seen her in 30 years! The babysitter remembered Holly as a little girl who talked nonstop and was very funny. Sounded about right to me.

The babysitter also told us about Holly's propensity to wet the bed. Then she talked about her mother. It was clear that Holly's mother was the one who had made up the story about finding Holly in a trash can because she was embarrassed to have to leave her at the orphanage. We asked many questions, specifically if there would be any way to find Holly's father. The answer was always something like "she had many suitors." It was evident that they either didn't know for sure or were not going to tell us anything else. I'm sure they didn't want to say directly that Holly's mother was likely a prostitute to survive during the war.

They did tell us that Holly's mom was an extremely nice and generous person. The stories were really interesting, and it was important for Holly to hear them. The main takeaway was that it was clear to everyone that her mother didn't want to give her up. That she really adored and loved Holly. The babysitter told us that her mom was adamant that Holly's needs be met and that she got the best care possible. Yes, Holly was a street child, so many of those kids were, but she was cared for, and her mother didn't want to let her go. I think it's important for an adopted person to hear that.

We were also able to visit her mom's gravesite. It was located behind the house, so we walked through a short alleyway that led to another row of modest homes. Behind them was a small cemetery with about a dozen coffins, all above ground. One of these was Holly's mom. We visited with the family and talked for a long time before returning to their house where they served us a wonderful meal. But the kicker for me was that Holly got to hear that her mother really didn't want to give her away, but she had been told that the North Vietnamese were going to come down and kill all the mixed children. So, it was a desperate act to ensure safety for her daughter.

We were told that her mother visited the orphanage every day, staying out of sight but checking on the welfare of her daughter from afar. Years later when she was dying, her last words were, "Holly coming?"

On the way back to our hotel, Holly and I talked about our conversation with her family and everything else that had gone on that day. I thought it helped both of us a lot because it partially filled in the blanks and put some context around Holly's early life. It also helped explain why her mother had to make such a difficult choice. And now we knew. She thought they were going to kill her daughter.

After college, Holly struggled a to find her way and manage her mental health. She eventually got into therapy and that seemed to help. Another of her coping mechanisms was her talent as a writer. She was able to express herself through words when her thoughts got too dark or negative. As Holly so succinctly described herself, "There are basically only four things you need to know about me. First, I'm a hummingbird on speed. Second, I'm drawn to misery. Third, I live to win the lottery. Finally, I'm a pathological liar."

One day in 2014, the phone rang while I was in my office. I saw that it was Holly's number. I'd learned early on that whenever she called, I needed to answer quickly because there was no telling what was going on. This time, she was uncharacteristically hysterical.

"Mom, I was just at the doctor and was told I have cervical cancer! I'm not sure what happened. I just thought it was an issue from the last pregnancy. It was supposed to be a routine visit. Now I'm not sure what to do!" she sobbed as I tried to process what she was saying.

"Holly, what do you mean? Just take a breath. Can I talk to your doctor?" I asked. Apparently, she had missed quite a few years of pap smears and a tumor had grown large enough that immediate action was needed.

"I have to go for more tests. I will call back soon."

We immediately flew her to Philadelphia for a second opinion and unfortunately the doctors at Penn confirmed the diagnosis. We tried to get her into a special study at the National Institute of Health (NIH) in Bethesda, MD, but we found out that she didn't qualify.

I remember driving home with her and trying to focus on the road. With all the information we'd been given, I knew in my gut that it meant she was going to die. I'm sure she had similar thoughts because our silence spoke volumes. We barreled down the road feeling numb and empty, knowing that our time together had become even more precious.

After weighing various options, Holly chose to return to Boise to be closer to her children while she underwent surgery and treatment. Holly was strong, a force to be reckoned with. So, I knew she would do her best to try and beat it. There was no denying that she was a true survivor. Holly's zest for life was unmatched. Sure, in making things work, she sometimes skirted the corners, but I had no doubt she would soldier on once she returned home.

When her cancer went into remission, I couldn't have been more grateful. Maybe I was wrong. Maybe she really would beat it. The doctors told her there was a 30% chance of recurrence, but for now she felt good, and her family was recovering from the lingering effects of fighting such a horrific disease.

Then, in typical Holly style, the other shoe dropped. I'd taken Holly and her two boys to the beach for a mini vacation to give her a chance to rest after the difficult few months she had endured. We were given access to a dear friend's cottage, and it was a lovely trip. One morning as I sat in the kitchen watching the boys play outside in the sand, Holly came downstairs. I knew instantly something was amiss. Her face was puffy, and it looked like she hadn't slept at all.

"Are you okay?" I asked. "Did you have too much to drink last night?"

"No, that's not it. I'm in trouble at work."

My chest tightened, and I thought about all the times I'd come to her rescue, usually financially, to get her out of a jam. This time, she'd been working at a distribution company and seemed to be doing well. She'd been there for years, and I'd long since relaxed into the fact that she had found a job that fulfilled her, professionally and financially. However, I knew that she would sometimes send me and other family members random boxes of products as gifts. I think it gave her a sense of satisfaction that she could finally do something for those who had helped her for so long. I had been concerned about how she could afford it, but I kept my mouth shut.

"Is it those products that you have been giving us?"

"Yes, I think that's part of it, but there's more. I got an email from them last night. I've been locked out of the company accounts. They've discovered some 'irregularities' in the accounting."

This was so Holly. We were in the middle of a lovely, relaxing vacation at the beach, and it was all about to crumble in front of me. No matter how many times it happened, the shock was as intense as the first one. While I was something of a handful as a young girl, I couldn't imagine getting into some of the messes that Holly seemed to land in with alarming regularity. Each time, I was assured it would be the last.

"Do you have any idea how much?" I asked, wondering what I'd have to cough up to get her back on track.

"I don't. They want to talk with me when I get home."

I took a deep breath and thought carefully before I spoke. "Holly, listen to me. This has to be the last time. I will help you as much as I can, but this is it. You have a family now. Your actions affect not just you but them as well."

"I know. I promise," she said as she hugged me tightly.

Somehow, we were able to get through that crisis. It was costly, and she had to pay restitution (correction, *I* had to pay), and I'm sure there were other details to which I was not privy. I felt horrible for everyone involved and was grateful when it was finally settled.

I have no doubt that the stress of those choices weighed heavily on her and her husband who helped navigate the legalities of her actions. I was glad when things settled down, and I hoped that Holly and her family were able to find happiness.

Only a few months later, Holly told me that the cancer had returned, and they were only giving her a year or two to live. I was crushed but remained outwardly hopeful for her sake. "You're a survivor," I told her. "If anyone can beat this, it's you. After all that you've been through—"

"Mom, it's okay. I'm going to fight it, but I'm also a realist. I even asked the doctor if the things I've done, if the guilt I feel, if maybe that somehow caused this...."

"Holly!"

"I know, but I had to ask. He said they had hoped the cancer had stabilized, but it hadn't."

"I'm here for you, Holly."

There was silence for a moment. "I know, Mom."

She fought valiantly, I think mostly because she didn't want to leave her husband and children behind, and we gathered at her house as often as possible. There was one instance where we were all there, most of the family, her husband and kids, and when I came in there was nowhere for me to sit. I found a small stool and pulled it over to her bedside. Once I sat down, I could just barely see over the bed. Maybe it was a child's stool, I'm not sure. Holly looked at me and said, "Mom, you've shrunk."

I don't know why that memory sticks with me, but it was so in line with her personality to say something lighthearted during such an intense time. I smiled at her comment but was preoccupied with making sure to protect her boys. We all knew it was only a matter of days, and when the time did come, we were at their house, and I herded everyone downstairs to the den to distract the children while the professionals took care of her.

My beloved daughter, Holly Thi Margolies Werth, passed away on May 3, 2016, in Boise, Idaho at the age of 48. The hospice workers told me several times that she was their favorite patient and kept them laughing until the end.

Holly was the writer in our family. People still talk about her gifted, hilarious tribute to my mother at her memorial service. This was my attempt at trying to capture her essence at Holly's celebration of life.

> *This is a tribute filled with love and etched in the ferocity that followed my beautiful daughter to the end of her life.*
>
> *Forty-two years ago, Ho Thi Tu Nga, a six-year-old from Vietnam became Holly Margolies a six-year-old New Yorker. Holly joined a small family, a single mom and an already fully integrated sister, Lee Heh, adopted several years earlier from Korea. The papers from the orphanage in Vietnam had seriously misrepresented the condition and health of Ho.*

Not noted was that she had been a street child, a pickpocket, stubborn, willful, beautiful, and riddled with worms, parasites, lice, skin sores, and rotting teeth. She had no language to convey her pain, only the ferocity that had enabled her to survive the six years of her ravaged life.

She entered her new world with all the ferocity of a bull in a China shop, dismantling everything and everyone in her path. Her little family of three soon changed with the addition of a dad, four new stepsisters, the birth of two brothers, and her parents' guardianship of three adopted Asian boys. This was a complicated home to navigate and grow in. Dinner guests would often hear Holly ask aloud, 'Are we going to adopt any of these people?' Her humor and ferocity often became audacity.

The ferocity that filled Holly was tamed in time as she quickly found language and began to feel safety, warmth, stability, and love, but it continued to inform her life. Holly was a survivor with a wit and humor that masked her early life. Until the age of 43 when she returned to Vietnam to visit her long-forgotten family, she lived with the belief of abandonment from her birth mother. The fact was that her mother had painfully and reluctantly taken her to an orphanage to avoid certain death, decreed by the soldiers from the North. Holly found that she had been deeply loved and from that knowledge, she was finally able to embrace all that she had been given by so many.

Holly excelled in school, was recruited for college for her lacrosse talent, and was a seeker of adventure in every corner of life... She graduated Friends Central, University of Pennsylvania, and Bryn Mawr College graduate school. She was a gifted writer, wrote for several television stations and publications. She was CFO for a wine distributor in Idaho without any degree in finance, signature Holly audacity.

Holly could bring people to scream with frustration or gales of laughter, all with a flourish. She was always just Holly.

Always seeking another adventure, she traveled to Sun Valley, Idaho, where she fell in love, settled down, and had two sons. She was the mother to her two sons, Trent and Jude, with the ferocity of a mama bear. Their early years would be as different from hers as the sun and the moon. Holly and Doug embraced their boys in a way denied to her.

Holly embraced her world with arms outstretched, humor, generosity, and great intellect. We who had the privilege of being touched by her beauty mourn her very sad ultimate passing. Cancer knows no justice in who it takes. Her trademark humor carried her through her terrible illness to the end.

When we knew her time here was limited, I asked how she would like to be remembered by me. She said, "You should begin my eulogy with 'Holly was always my favorite child.'

Every day since she passed, I've made a point to wear something of hers. It may be a sweater or just a small piece of jewelry, but it's a ritual that brings me a sense of peace. It's my way of keeping her close to me.

PART II

Timeless Lessons

CHAPTER 11

On the Frontlines of Motherhood

*You must learn to be still in the midst of activity and to be
vibrantly alive in repose.*

– INDIRA GANDHI

I'VE LEARNED HEAPS ABOUT MOTHERHOOD through my own varied experiences. And I've compiled some of my favorite timeless parenting stories. That's why there's no mention of transitory distractions that have taunted parents throughout the decades like TVs, pinball machines, video games, tablets, and cell phones. There will always be some type of technology designed to improve our lives and distract our children. My hope with sharing more of my adventures in motherhood, and those of people I've interviewed, is to show that while the circumstances may change and the distractions become more intrusive, parenting challenges are universal.

As a journalist, I've always been fascinated with how others see the world, especially when it comes to family. Throughout my career, I've met and interviewed many types of parents and family units. I also frequently consulted trusted therapists and psychologists to better understand those experiences.

Taking a look at the various ways we become a mother helps to show us how our experiences compare and the similarities we all invariably share. We may not follow the same parenting styles, but our goals are the same, to raise our children to be the best they can be.

⚬❀⚬

THE SINGLE MOTHER

There are many reasons that a woman becomes a single parent. The widow, the divorced woman, the unmarried mother, and the single adoptive mother are all in the position of raising their children without a father. I was a single mother by choice, and I know both the joy and the loneliness that brings. I can remember the times when I wanted to say, "I've had it. Take over while I get some breathing room," or "Isn't that cute? Did you hear what she just said?" But there was no one to share either of these times with me.

When I decided to adopt, I decided on a little girl. I felt that because I was a woman, I would better understand the needs and development of a daughter. It was a traditional view, but one that made sense. But women also successfully raise their sons alone. Often, they have no choice. While many of the problems of single mothering are the same, there are problems which are unique to each type of single mother.

The widow has to help her children understand death. The death of a father can seem like the ultimate abandonment. There is a grieving process that must be managed. This time can be difficult because the mother is going through the same process. Children often have mixed feelings about their parents, and that can complicate grieving. Many children feel guilty about the death of a parent because they have thought or said harmful words and may not have made amends.

A psychiatrist told me about one of his patients who sought family counseling after her husband's sudden death. He said that her reactions and those of her son were not uncommon, and that even when the death was an expected one, the same feelings often exist.

"I know Johnny's angry," said the woman when she called. "I know he's sad. I can see the suppressed anger in the way he holds himself. He can't express it."

It's very natural for a child and the mother to be angry about death. During the therapy sessions, the doctor encouraged both the mother and the child to voice their love and their anger. During the final session, the mother and son held each other while they cried.

When Brenda's husband died, she was left to raise four children from the ages of ten to twenty. "The two oldest children handled themselves very well and went through the grieving process with few problems. They understood what their father's cancer had done to him. The two youngest were ten and eleven and hadn't known their father very much when he wasn't ill since it developed early in their lives."

They understood illness, but they couldn't understand death. "My ten-year-old, Johnny, reverted to infantile behavior. He began bedwetting and wanting to sit on my lap. The eleven-year-old, Melissa, went from a sunny disposition to a morose one. I was also angry about the abandonment, and we spent many long hours talking to each other about what the death meant to us as a family. It might have taken us four years to recover from facing death."

As we all know, divorces that involve children are quite common. There is often bitterness on the part of the divorced partners, and that can spill over to the children. Sometimes, these children are made to feel one parent is right and the other is wrong. Children may equate "Mommy and Daddy don't love each other anymore" with "Mommy and Daddy don't love me."

"My girls were hurt when their father didn't show up to take them out like he'd promised," said one mother I know. "It has been something they had been looking forward to, and I had been looking forward to being alone. I was angry, and I let the girls know it. When he called to explain and it was valid, the girls refused to listen. At first, I was happy because it meant they were on my side. Then I began to see their schoolwork suffer, and my oldest began to run wild. I was forced to look at what my anger was doing to them. Children shouldn't be forced to take sides. It took years of therapy to help me, and my girls, get back on a healthy track."

A friend named Carol told me, "Soon after our divorce was final, my husband left. Neither the girls nor I heard from him for two years. He didn't pay child support either. The girls knew I was responsible for their support, and it worked out fairly well, though there were times when extra money would have come in handy."

Unmarried women, specifically, have to face the stigma that society attaches to them and their children. A father of record, and of fact, seems to be vital in the minds of many people. While things are changing, often the children of unmarried mothers are made to feel shame because of their position.

I think we can all agree that the term "illegitimate" should be banned from the English language when it's used as an adjective with "child." For the mother, so should "unwed." The reactions of the public to unmarried mothers were brought home to me as a result of one of my earlier reporting assignments.

In March of 1972, my daily duty was to cover Princess Alexandria of Greece and Tricia Nixon as they visited a school for developmentally challenged children in Valhalla, New York. To help the story come alive, I wanted to interview one of the students. The girl I chose took the microphone and turned the tables.

"How old are you?" she asked.

"Twenty-nine," I answered.

"Do you have any children?"

"One little girl," I said.

"Do you have a husband?"

"No."

"Oh, my," she said. "How many telephones do you have?"

When we returned to the studio and put the story together, this interview was the magic moment that brought it all together. After the airing, the station received a lot of mail, most of it either praising or condemning me.

The story of my life.

※

THE ADOPTIVE MOTHER

In most states, there is a waiting period before the adoption becomes final. This time period can seem long, and often there is an underlying fear on the part of the child and the parent that something will go wrong. Children may test their parents because often they have learned to distrust rather than to trust. The child may initially react to the new home with tears and tantrums.

I know because that is the way Holly reacted. She wouldn't stay in bed. She woke up screaming because of nightmares. She hated to wear shoes. I never knew what would trigger one of her tantrums. On top of all this, she understood very little English at first, and I didn't speak the Vietnamese language. I learned, "Does it hurt?" "Do you have to GO to the bathroom?" "Are you hungry?" Those phrases became useless quickly. It was a slow process compounded by Lee Heh's resentment of the amount of my time Holly needed.

I remember one evening when I came home from work after a particularly exhausting day to find the girls quarreling.

"I'm tired. I've had it," I shouted. "When you settle your quarrel, you can come and talk to me." I headed for my room and laid on my bed.

Soon afterwards, the girls came into my room, "It was my jar, and she knew it," said Lee Heh, showing me a small jar of makeup.

"I take Lee Heh's jar," said Holly. "Couldn't find mine. I take Lee Heh's jar to take it for mine. I sorry."

"It's over," I said. "Let's talk about something else."

"Talk." Lee Heh pouted. "You don't have time to talk to me."

I sat up in bed. "Lee Heh, you know better."

"She wants all your time."

"We have nearly two hours every night after Holly goes to bed."

"But then you're on the telephone."

"Only when it's an emergency—something to do with my work." Lee Heh began to cry. "What's wrong?" I asked.

"You were yelling at me. We never fought before Holly came."

"Sweetie, we have to learn to live together. It's a three-way street."

"It's a traffic jam," she mumbled.

I touched her hair. Holly was already beside me. "Things have changed this year. You're stronger and Holly's softer. Come on the bed with us. We're a family."

We were a family with all the problems that come with family living. Our problems seemed exaggerated because my daughters had arrived with their own personalities and influenced by their own cultural backgrounds.

When I adopted my girls, I tried to provide them with dual heritage. First, there was their racial/cultural background. Then came the American heritage they fell into. When they arrived, I knew very little about their upbringing except in a general way. I was working blindly and with faulty information.

Sometimes information is withheld about an adopted child because it is feared the adopting family will reject the child. Other times, there is no information available. I know I wouldn't have rejected either of my daughters, but if I had had more information, I would have been better prepared for living with them. When people adopt a child with a physical handicap, the evidence is usually obvious and often a solution can be found. Emotional trauma is more difficult to unravel. I was sure both my daughters had experienced some level of emotional scarring.

Pictures of the past are very important. Children like to look at pictures of themselves when they were younger. Adults do also. I know I do because these pictures trigger memories, especially at the stage of my life, happy and sad.

A New York psychiatrist friend of mine introduced me to a woman named Janet who was a mother, a nurse, and a writer, a poet to be exact. He told me she had a wide variety of experience with children, both her own and children who belonged to others. She and I talked about our children, and I learned that she had also adopted a daughter, a biracial child who had lived in three foster homes and had been abused before she came to live with Janet at the age of nearly four. I told Janet the story of my girls and the pictures of their past.

A look of dismay crossed her face. "Veronica's life began when she was nearly four and she came to live with us. I wish we had pictures of her before she arrived. I often wonder what she looked like as a baby. I remember one day when she came home from school and asked for a picture for the Beautiful Baby contest. I got out the album her godparents had assembled when she first came to live with us. She wouldn't take one of those pictures to school because they weren't of a baby. I wish social agencies would realize how important pictures can be. I have a cousin who is a foster mother, and she takes pictures of her foster children. When they leave her house, they take a record with them."

Not only are pictures important but knowing what happened to your child and an honest appraisal of the child's behavior is meaningful. When an adoptive family is faced with a total change in behavior from what was reported, feelings of guilt arise. "What are we doing wrong?" they ask. "The report says she sleeps and eats well. She is a quiet child who amuses herself." This picture doesn't fit the child who has nightmares, temper tantrums, and who only eats certain foods.

At dinner the first night, Janet's daughter threw a tantrum when they tried to make her eat roast beef. After the storm settled, Janet received this explanation from her daughter. "Big peoples eat meat. Kids eat hot dogs and hamburgers." The report said she ate anything.

Holly was afraid to sleep alone at night, though the report said she slept well. In Vietnam, ghosts are part of the culture. People often sleep in groups for protection from ghosts. I wish I had known this when she arrived. It would have helped me understand her better.

Another thing an adoptive mother must face are these words, "You 're not my real mother." Lee Heh wanted me to be her mother so badly she asked early on if she could crawl inside me and become my "real" child. Not so with Holly who chose the opposite route. Those words can be used by adoptive children when there is a conflict of wills or a disciplinary situation. They are often used with the words, "I don't have to listen to you." The words sting; they hurt no matter how prepared one may be. And it's hard not to let it show.

While the sentiment "you're not my real mother" is literally true, an adoptive mother has generally made a serious emotional commitment to her adoptive child. She feels she *is* the child's mother, just as she is the mother of her biological children. How do you explain to a child that mothering is an emotional experience?

I remember once when I watched a talk show, one of the guests was a mother with an eclectic family like ours. The interviewer, with all the finesse of an aardvark said, "which ones are your natural children and which ones are not?" The mother very coolly replied, "I forget." My sentiments exactly.

One afternoon, Holly called home from a friend's house. "Mom, I don't feel well. I'm dizzy and I have a headache. I don't think I can go with the family tonight."

"Do you want me to call the doctor?" I asked. "I'll come right over and pick you up."

"No," she said. "I see two aspirin that will help me. Can I go roller skating?"

"You know we have a family thing planned."

"I don't want to go. I want to be with my friends."

For the next twenty minutes, we went back and forth. Finally, Holly shouted, "I don't have to listen to you! You're not my real mother!"

I reacted to the pain that statement caused. "I don't care what you do."

That wasn't the truth of course. Nor were the words she used. I cared very much what she did, and she knew I was her mother. She also knew how much her words could hurt me, and I responded to those words with my own. What I wanted to say was, "I am your mother because I care. I am not your biological mother. I want you to go with the family because while you need independence, you also need the security of knowing you belong. Learning these two things is part of growing up."

Those words wouldn't have worked either. I'm not sure there was a winner in that situation. It was a quarrel with no resolve.

I have been a lifelong advocate for adoption, domestic and abroad, and have hosted or spoken at many events over the years. In 2011, Susan and I were part of the International Forum on Intercountry Adoption sponsored in part by Holt

International. President Bill Clinton was kind enough to write a letter of support that was included in the program.

WILLIAM JEFFERSON CLINTON

March 15, 2011

Hillary and I are delighted to share in the celebration of Holt International's 55th anniversary and to acknowledge your important international forum on intercountry adoption.

Hillary was privileged to be named honorary chair of Holt International while serving as First Lady, and both of us have admired your tremendous work over the last decades. You've been instrumental in uniting thousands of families and saving so many children from a childhood without loving parents.

We especially applaud the adult adoptees who will bring their unique and valuable experience to the discussions. While they are living examples of the benefits of intercountry adoption over institutionalization, they also have a keen awareness of the obstacles these families face, and the work that remains to help children and parents alike through a lifetime filled with both challenges and joy.

I'd be remiss in addressing this celebration of families if I didn't mention how wonderful it is that your gala is being hosted by Marjorie Margolies, whom Hillary and I have known and admired for years and whose son Marc we welcomed into our family last year. Families do indeed come together in many ways, and I can think of no more inspiring individual than Marjorie to lead the celebration.

As you gather in work and celebration, I hope you find the same kind of inspiration you bring to those of us who admire your steadfastness, your professionalism, and your dedication to uniting vulnerable children with loving parents.

Sincerely,

Bill Clinton

THE STEPMOTHER

What do you think when you hear the word "stepmother?" The word has conjured up bad feelings for centuries. In fairy tales, it was always the mean, cruel stepmother who harmed the children or kept the father from paying attention to them. *Cinderella. Hansel and Gretel. Snow White.* When those tales were written, the chances of children having a stepmother were high. Women frequently died in childbirth and men remarried to provide mothers for their children, and to have more children. Over a hundred years ago, a man on average would have two or three wives in their lifetime. Considering the fairy tales, is it any wonder we react negatively to that word?

When I talked to a licensed therapist about the problems of stepmothers, she said there was too much emphasis on making the stepmother into an instant mother. She said many people considered the role of stepmother as a problem. It should instead be considered a situation of unfamiliarity.

Most first-time stepmothers will practice caution rather than rushing headlong into parenting action. That is the usual way of dealing with the unfamiliar. It can be damaging to immediately say, "I'm your mother. You're my child." Any relationship takes time to build and establish. The interaction between a stepmother and her stepchildren is a very different relationship for which both are often not prepared. Of course, much depends on the age of the child. A very young one will often enjoy being held and may form a relationship with the stepmother more quickly than the older child.

Louise, a friend of mine, lost her mother at only a year old. She was three when her father remarried. She called her stepmother "Mom." "I don't think of her as my stepmother. She's the only mother I remember. She's, well, she's my mother. As an adult,

I still spend two weeks visiting her each summer and enjoy it."

But stepmothers aren't always acquired through the death of a mother. When a divorced man remarries, his children have a stepmother. That's what happened in my situation. Sometimes there is resentment of this woman, and the children consider her an interloper. Sometimes the stepmother resents the time her husband spends with the children of a former marriage.

"We never have a weekend alone," one stepmother told me. "Every vacation must be planned around what his kids want to do."

She may have a valid point, or she could be overreacting. There is usually room for compromise in those situations.

Claire, another friend, calls hers a blended family. "I don't think of the kids as being his or mine, but ours. I also try to consider the other mother when I am dealing with my stepchildren and attempt to maintain as much consistency between my rules and hers as I can. Children will manipulate. I try very hard not to give them that opportunity."

When I married Ed, I became a stepmother. His daughters were frequently in our home, and I enjoyed having them there. There's a difference between being a mother and being a stepmother. A stepmother has a lesser investment in her stepchildren than their biological mother does. This doesn't' make it harder or easier, just challenging.

The toughest part for me was working to keep from becoming an ogre. I didn't want my four stepdaughters to feel that I was coming down on them about their habits, manners, or attitudes. It is impossible to have the same exact values in any two households, so everyone must learn to adjust. I had to be a little looser and a little more understanding with them. Then the other children would say I was not being fair to them. They may have been right, but I felt that what I was doing was right for me in my role as the stepmother.

I talked to my stepchildren and told them I had some basic rules. I think it's always good to set some kind of baseline rules, but I tried to keep mine to a minimum. Then I tried to handle problems as they came up. If there was a conflict between what they were allowed to do at home and what I liked done in my home, I tried to let them know neither way was right or wrong, but that their mother and I were two different people. I just wouldn't play the game of "I'm right and she's wrong." Rather, I tried to say, "In this house, we do it this way."

I was fortunate because I had a good relationship with Ed's first wife. She was a kind person, and we talked to each other often. We didn't agree on everything, but who does? We did agree that we both wanted the best for those four girls. What I really wanted for them was to feel that they were welcome and could spend as much time there as they liked. Luckily, both Holly and Lee Heh were also always welcomed at their stepsisters' house, a lovely arrangement.

One time, I was watching one of my stepdaughters play with one of my sons, Marc. He ran to her, and she picked him up and hugged him. The sound of their laughter filled me with joy. That's what I tried to achieve, a place where all the children could laugh.

The four girls, by the way, did not call Marc and Andrew their half-brothers. They were just plain ole brothers. When one came back from camp one summer, we talked about our melded family. She admitted that she had a lot of fun with the concept at camp. When she was asked, "How many kids are in your family?" she told them, "Are you ready for this one...?"

When I talked to the therapist, he told me that life does not often flow smoothly for mothers and stepmothers, in his experience. Sometimes the gulf in values is too great. He told me about one of his patients who was placed in a very difficult position in her role as stepmother. She had two stepdaughters, and the oldest always wore a sweater over her clothes. She took the girls shopping one day and told them they could select what they wanted. Suddenly, the older child lit up. She chose very stylish clothes and discarded her sweaters and what appeared to be hand-me-downs. "Thank you," she said. "I've always been ashamed of my clothes, but my mom doesn't have enough money to buy us new clothes. We go thrift shopping sometimes. I still don't like that you married my dad, but you did see that there was something I needed. I don't love you, but I'll try to respect you."

I think it's hard to say stepmothers want their stepchildren or even their own children to always love them. For me, respect was almost as valuable because love often followed. While Ed and I were married, we attended the wedding of one of his daughters, and of course his ex-wife was there. I insisted that we sit together to avoid the awkward division that can often follow a divorce. That way we could avoid any tension and celebrate the special day despite the divorce in the room.

The bride came over to me in the middle of the reception and pulled me aside. She said, "I really want to thank you for making sure everyone was together, and things were not awkward and uncomfortable."

That's just one of the jobs of a mother.

-❧-

THE SPONSORING MOTHER

When I became a sponsoring mother, I was following in my mother's footsteps...in my own way. When I was in college, I met Rosemary. Her mother had died, and her father had moved back to Lebanon. She wanted to stay in the U.S. My parents agreed to act as her sponsor.

Then there was Vicky, the one I'd met in Spain on the "Experiment for International Living." My parents sponsored her and her husband's entrance into the United States. She practically became a daughter. My parents were the only grandparents her children really knew.

Soon after I was married, we ended up not just sponsoring a child or young adult but entire families. Even though there were adults involved, two distinct aspects of mothering were necessary—nurturing and teaching. The Ha family was our first family unit. Mr. and Mrs. Ha were teachers. They had a twenty-year-old daughter and a ten-year-old son. The Has were Chinese and had fled from China to North Vietnam, and then South Vietnam. They spoke no English, and Mr. Ha had cataracts. We built a place for them at our home, and they stayed for two years. They were followed by a Korean couple with two children, a Mennonite woman who had married a Black man, and then there was Mrs. Suu, her biological son and her two nephews.

When sponsoring a family, there were guidelines that had been established by the American Refugee Committee. There were certain governmental requirements to be fulfilled as well. The children, as well as the adults, had to have Social Security numbers. To receive their card, they had to bring their I-94 cards to the Social Security Office. That card was their permit to enter the country and provided them with eligibility for refugee assistance programs. Children between the ages of six and sixteen had to be registered for school.

Many of those refugee families had serious medical problems because they had often spent months in harsh camps. They had been traumatized leaving their homes and escaping their home country. While the U.S. was a refuge, all the new experiences could give them culture shock.

Most of the time when sponsored families lived with us, they took care of their own children. Since they were not my children,

I was not involved in the childrearing process. Things were different with the Suu family. Mrs. Suu and I shared the cooking and other household tasks. Her son, Vu, and my son, Marc, became fast friends, but sometimes the cultural differences were quite evident.

Vu was the first son. In the Vietnamese family, that had special meaning. His mother waited on him, and he expected it. That was certainly contrary to my belief that teaching independence was part of a mother's responsibility to her child.

One day, my parents brought Vu a blackboard with chalk and erasers. Vu gave it back because it was "no good." In translation, he told us, "Guns, cars, airplanes, and tanks are proper presents for boys." My parents were surprised and hurt, but we were all learning. Slowly, Vu began to adapt and accept his new culture.

Part of my sponsoring mother role was to help them make the transition to living in this country. Children usually learn the customs faster than the adults. They also learn the language with more ease, especially when there are other children around.

Vu was only a few years older than Marc, so they were frequently together, and the cultural transference worked both ways. In Vietnam at the time, there was no indoor plumbing in most homes. So Vu squat on the toilet seat to use the bathroom. Following his lead, Marc did the same thing. That meant they had to completely undress and redress each time. My mother saw Marc following Vu's lead, and she became concerned. I told her, "I promise you that he won't be doing that by the time he gets to college."

I'm not sure she found it as amusing as I did.

—❀—

THE BIOLOGICAL MOTHER

Marc's birth made me a biological mother. I call him my first bio-kid. There was something special about the experience of pregnancy; emotional ties are often formed with the baby long before birth. It was that way for me. Giving birth was also something special. I had finally done what people subtly and not so subtly had been after me to do for years. I had gotten married and had a baby. Not long after we were married, during an interview, I was asked if we would like more children.

"A baby?" I replied.

Lee Heh looked at me in shock. "Are you going to have a baby when you have six or eight other children?" she asked.

"Not in the next twenty minutes," I assured her. That was in January of 1976. Marc was born in December of 1977.

In a family like ours with such an assortment of inter-related children, the presence of one more didn't seem like it would make much difference, I thought when I found out that I was pregnant. To me, a bio-baby meant another child to love and cherish. Most of the children accepted my pregnancy as just another event in the controlled chaos that was our family. Lee Heh was the exception.

For seven months, she was distant and even punitive. I remember when Ed's Congressional class had a baby shower for him. We brought the presents home and put them in the sitting room next to our bedroom. Lee Heh came in. I was asleep. She piled the packages neatly and quietly, and slowly began to cry.

I woke and wasn't sure what to do. I asked if she'd like to talk. She said "no," and I felt I shouldn't push the issue. The next day, I called my friend Helen and asked how I should handle the situation. "You did the right thing. She's crying for the baby who was and the baby who's coming. She's crying for the childhood she remembers and the childhood she doesn't remember. She's crying for the baby she wants and the baby she fears. She'll be all right."

That turned out to be good advice. On the day we brought Marc home, he became the most important thing in her life. His face lit up when he saw her enter the room, and hers did the same. To this day, they remain close friends.

When there are other children in the home, whether they're biological, adopted, or any other variety, the coming baby can stir up mixed emotions. Knowing the other children may not feel the same about the coming baby as you do can help when dealing with their feelings. Any new addition to the group would create change, and it was my job to stay alert for those changes in them and in me.

The arrival of Marc was a meaningful experience for me because I decided that I wanted to breastfeed, even if only for a short time. I had read that during that period of time, the mother passes to the baby all of her acquired immunities. After six weeks, I would return to work. I had asked my obstetrician, "When am I going to wean this child?"

"You are not," he said.

"Dr., I am not taking this child to his bar mitzvah like this."

"If anybody can, I figure it would be you." Then he went on to tell me about a pump that I could use during the day when I couldn't get home to nurse. I bought one and learned how to use it. Before I returned to work, I also bought a small Styrofoam cooler, the kind that holds a six-pack of beer. Then I got two of those packs that can be frozen to keep things cold. During the day, I pumped when and where I could. Often, I would ask the camera crew how long it would take to get the needed shots. Those ten or fifteen minutes were spent in the nearest ladies' room or emergency van or empty office pumping and putting the milk in bottles for Marc the next day. My friend in the newsroom called the cooler my "two pack" and one of my fellow reporters dubbed me "The Real Dairy Queen."

One day I was giving a talk to wives of newly elected Congressmen in the House and Senate about what to expect from the media. The guard at the Capitol looked at my cooler and demanded to examine it. I handed it to him. He opened it and pulled out the pump. "What is this?" he asked.

"A breast pump," I replied.

He nearly broke it in his haste to put it back in the cooler. As I walked away, I heard him say to his colleague, "You're not going to believe this one!"

-❊-

THE FOSTER MOTHER

Ok, I was never a foster mother, but I thought it important to cover the topic. I really feel I would have had a hard time being a part of the foster parent system. I don't think I had the temperament for that very special kind of mothering. I would have been psychologically unable to give up a child once I had begun to love the little one. In my case, I was a sucker for children and love for them came easily. I would have been torn apart when it was time for them to leave. Foster home placement was generally short term. I have always admired foster mothers (and foster parents in general), and during my news career I did many stories about them.

As a news reporter, I often saw the tragedy of foster parenting. There was the story about a woman who had been a foster mother of two for four years. She was given ten days' notice that the children would be removed from her home. She was told that her arthritis prevented her from properly caring for them. She took her case to court. According to the children, she was a kind, understanding mother, one they wanted to stay with.

"This mommy is not a mommy with a strap. The last one I was with was," one of them said.

At that time, more than 300,000 children were in foster care situations in the U.S. I found with those stories that sometimes the rights of the children were overlooked and, in some cases, totally ignored.

I covered the joint House and Senate Subcommittee on select education where they heard testimony from experts in the field of foster care. The committee heard story after story of how poorly the system was (or wasn't) working. A thirty-year-old woman had been in nineteen foster homes as a child. She and her sister were separated and abused in their foster homes.

Other stories I did addressed the group approach to foster care. At first, group homes were established with married couples as house parents, but that didn't work because most of the kids were running from just that sort of living situation. Another story about foster homes involved women who were foster mothers to babies who were born to women in prison or other institutions.

I seldom saw the beautiful stories of women who loved their foster children while they were in their home, and those who continued to love and care for children after they left. I'm sure there were more happy stories than tragedies, at least I hope so, but tragedy made its way into the headlines more easily then. I suppose that hasn't changed much over the years.

A woman named Virginia raised eleven children of her own and quite a few foster kids. She tried to count them one day, but they all became mixed up. "They're all my children when they're living in my home and many times even after they leave." Some of them were placed in her home through agencies and others were friends of her children who dropped in to get away from a bad situation at their home. Some of them had aged out of the system, but they were still in need of her guidance.

"When someone's hungry, you feed them," she said. "Around here, there's always a trick to stretching a meal. Add another potato or throw more spaghetti in the pot. When someone needs a bed, you find a place for them, even if it's a sleeping bag on the floor. When they need someone to care, you care, and when they need someone to listen, you listen to their problems. They can stay as long as they don't bring trouble into my house—a lot of fighting, refusing to help with the chores, or by not trying to better themselves."

At that time, she had four of her own children living at home. "The youngest is a foster child we adopted. He was just a few months old when he came to our home. My husband has a hard time letting the kids go, and he said if anyone took this one, he'd have a nervous breakdown. We have three permanent foster children, and one who may become permanent if we can find the proper help for her. My grandson also lives with us. He and my adopted son think they're brothers, and we can't dissuade them."

Her grown foster children even came back to visit her and brought their wives and babies. One day, three of them arrived on a surprise visit. She threw more food in the kettle and found places for them to spend the night. They sat up and talked long into the evening. "The nicest thing they kept saying was, 'Mommy hasn't changed a bit.'"

❦

THE WORKING MOTHER

I was always one of the mothers who liked to work, and naturally I know many women in this category. When I talk to them, they all mention that it gives them a sense of worth to contribute financially to the household. My friend, Lois, was being paid for work she did as a volunteer.

"Things changed," she said. "My attitudes and the attitudes of my coworkers changed. When I was a volunteer, if I didn't feel like showing up, no one said anything. After I had children, if I didn't go to work, I'd better have a good reason. My opinion of myself has changed. The reaction of my children surprised me. They were proud of Mom. That's another reason for feeling good, setting an example for them."

A writer friend named Janet returned to work part-time as a nurse after a twenty-year hiatus. Nursing is a draining job, emotionally and physically, and I asked her why she continued to write as well.

"For a couple of reasons. As an example, for my children, to show them a person can succeed and enjoy a job that is not their first choice. Nursing is a second choice with me, but writing is a chancy career unless you're hired for steady work. I began writing as a break from being 'Mommy.' I didn't want my children to think being a mother was all I could do. The writing was never looked on by them as a job because I worked at home. There was also a selfish reason for returning to nursing. Writing is a lonely profession, and I needed to be with people more. I can write sixteen hours a day, especially if I'm wrestling with a poem."

Not too long ago, when children were asked if they wanted their mother to work, they responded with "no" (plenty of husbands, too). Thankfully, things have changed. One of my children's friends even told her mother to lie when asked if she worked. "Tell them you have a job, Mom. All of the other mothers work."

Working mothers need to have a support system to back them up. I would never have been able to continue to work and to be a mother if it hadn't been for my parents' willingness to step in and take over for me when I had a late-night assignment, or when I had a date. I realized just how much they helped out when Lee Heh and I moved to New York. I missed having them able to arrive at a moment's notice. But shortly after I arrived in New York, I began to build other support systems.

Nothing ever replaced the devotion of my parents, but my New York friends were super. A couple and their children in my old apartment building became a second family and they were willing to stay with Lee Heh if I needed them. The Fosters were incredible to us. I can remember calling them one morning at 3:00 a.m. because two ships had collided under the Verrazano Bridge, and I had been called to come in to cover it. I took the girls up to sleep with our neighbors. Neither one knew where she was when she woke up in the morning.

I met a wonderful young teacher on a story one day. It turned out that she lived in my building on Sutton Place. She and Holly became fast friends. Holly didn't know her name, only her apartment number, 4B. So, she was forever saying, "I'm going to see 4B" or "4B is sick today."

An understanding kindergarten teacher solved another dilemma. When Holly arrived, I enrolled her in first grade, but she had difficulty adjusting. One minute she would be sweet, and the next, fighting and crying. The teacher suggested she go back to kindergarten. *But that's only half a day*, I thought. *What would I do with her from noon until the babysitter picked her up?* Lee Heh suggested a daycare center. I called a friend who ran one, and fortunately, a teacher there said that Holly could attend both sessions of kindergarten.

The coming of Holly made me realize the value of an extended family. And also to realize that in today's society, where family members often live at a distance from each other, that an extended family can include friends and other people who can in some way help a working mother from spreading herself too thin. By the way, I'm not sure that's possible. I was forever on "overload" (still am) and always saying the words, "you're no superwoman" to myself.

This new look at the family structure of today also showed me something else. A giant generation gap often exists between our children and seniors. I think the children lose out because of this. There is a continuity of life which they miss when they only see seniors from a distance. When you think of it, most of us spend the majority of our waking hours with people close to our age.

I did stories on this very subject. There has always been a special kind of communication between grandparent and grandchild. A group of children from the Hawthorne Middle School in Yonkers, New York, had a program called "The Generation Bridge." At least two times a month they visited the Hebrew Home for the Aged in Riverdale where they tried to close the generation gap. The average age of the adults there was 83 and the students was 13. There were no holds barred and both generations learned to respect others' opinions.

Another story I did was about foster grandparent programs which were thriving throughout the country at the time. One group of foster grandparents I wrote about brought patience and understanding to children in hospitals and institutions. To be one of those grannies, you had to be sixty or older, be below the poverty level, and have experience with children. While they were paid a small amount for their transportation and meals, they got as much from the program as the children they helped.

When Lee Heh arrived, my grandmother was still alive. She was sick and much of the family had difficulty dealing with it. Lee Heh knew instantly to show courtesy and respect to the older woman. Lee Heh was one of the only ones who felt comfortable touching and caressing her. She was so gentle and kind and sometimes even crawled onto my grandmother's bed. My grandmother, like many, thought I was nuts when I first adopted, but at that time she began saying, "Where's the little girl?"

As a career woman and a journalist, I was inspired by the

goings-on in all the newsrooms I'd worked in and encouraged by the success of my first book to write another. I decided to write a book about women in television and chose to use fiction to better dramatize what lives are like in the volatile, male-dominated business of TV news. I've spent most of my adult life as a TV journalist, and the 1980's fiction characters in *The "Girls" in the Newsroom* are very real to me.

They faced one hurdle after another as they sought to be taken seriously. Have things changed? Travel 38 years into the year 2021, and the so-called "girls" in the newsroom are now correctly referred to as "women" and their numbers have grown dramatically. A 2020 Syracuse University/Radio Television News Directors Association (RTNDA) study reports that 44% of television newsroom staffers are female. Worldwide, according to the 6th Global Media Monitoring Project, the percentage of women involved in traditional media is 25%, but the numbers are greater within digital platforms.

Despite the significant growth in numbers. Many of the same hurdles continue to exist. The "Me Too" movement in the media is a stark reminder of this fact, and "Me Too" can take many forms. One female executive with 35 years of experience told me several incidents continue to haunt her.

I will never forget seeing a young female reporter candidate literally jump up during the interview and run from the news director's office out the door and into her car. The news director had a rep, so I had good reason to believe he had likely acted inappropriately. I even questioned him before the interview was over. He squirmed and denied. I called the candidate several times as to what had happened, but I never saw or heard from her again. Why did I tell his boss of my suspicions? For two reasons: I didn't have any hard evidence, and he would have laughed it off as a 'boys will be boys' kind of thing. That was very common in my career.

Another reason so many women avoid coming forward is the simple fact that a serious complaint is a deal breaker for most companies regardless of its merit. In other words, good luck getting promoted or hired elsewhere. When I started writing this book, I asked thirty women in the business if they had ever been a victim of sexual harassment. Most said they had witnessed it but had not experienced it. Later, I heard from several of them via discrete phone calls offering an experience but insisting their name could not be used.

A distinguished and popular male newscaster who anchored a Washington news station for 10 years said, "There's definite discrimination, but it's become so subtle, and those who practice it have become so sophisticated in the execution of it that it's difficult to make a clear, verifiable case." He added that "women and minorities get fewer chances to fail than do white men."

"What worries me the most," said a female correspondent in Washington, "is that you can work like a dog, be a terrific reporter, and do a great job on a story, but if the way you look is unacceptable to one executive, all the other factors don't matter."

Another agreed, "For a woman in TV news, how you look is 50% more important than what you say."

Journalist and TV producer Clare Crawford-Mason once quipped that if she ever found a world leader lying dead on the floor, she'd hide his body, run to put on makeup and do her hair, and then go on camera to tell the story. In another example, newswoman Jessica Savitch put less focus on her appearance and more on the story as she raced into the newsroom to become the first person to break the news. Almost immediately, calls poured into the station commenting on her tousled appearance with no mention of the impressive scoop.

Meanwhile, a male reporter without a tie, his sleeves rolled up, glasses low on his nose, and hair a bit askew is seen as a physical representation of hard work. Let's face it, a woman in the TV news then or now couldn't get away with the ears of Ted Koppel, Hugh Downs' hairline, or the smugness of countless men—all well-respected journalists, but they didn't have to worry nearly as much about their looks. And the audience was far more forgiving. There's no denying that as we age, men become venerable, and women become vulnerable.

I am thankful I did not have to deal with the new age of digital information. Today's journalists, regardless of gender, now face a constant barrage of commentary on their looks and their work. This has also led to serious cases of stalking, bullying, and much more.

According to my friend and highly respected former news director at WPVI-TV in Philadelphia Carla Carpenter, the changes that have occurred in the industry are certainly encouraging. In fact, according to RTNDA 36% of news stations have female news directors, but only 19% have female general managers. We still have much to do in the quest to achieve equal female and minority representation, but unfortunately, the industry is not unique.

An administrative assignment editor said, "TV is no different than any other place in society. Women our age simply won't put up with sex discrimination anymore."

If she's right, and I tend to agree with her, that the TV news-room simply reflects male attitudes in general toward women, then the reasons for any lingering, albeit subtle, vestiges of sex discrimination in the newsroom are more clearly understood.

Another added, "Sex discrimination is subconscious and unconscious, not deliberate. All the important decisions on TV news are often made by men, mostly men who are half a generation or more older than we are. They were raised to think that women were prettier than men, and that they're supposed to treat men differently from women. That's a fact, not a criticism."

A successful female anchor confided in me that she didn't feel women were taken as seriously by men as they should be. She was told early in her career that she'd never make it as an anchor because she was "too intelligent." One of her early male bosses told her, "Women should be perky and upbeat. It makes viewers feel better. Leave the serious emotions to the men."

A news producer in Philadelphia for almost twenty years said, "When I became an assignment editor, a technician told me 'I'm not taking orders from a female. I don't care who she is.'"

Men in the engineering end of television often assume that a woman does not have the ability to understand complex technical matters. A news editor in Washington recalled being interviewed for a technical job at ABC. She was told the problem was that she'd have to have a First Class FCC license. She produced hers. "They hired thirteen of us," she said, "nine men and four women. All four women had First Class licenses. Only one of the men did."

A male field producer in Washington said, "I don't find much sex discrimination at my network, but there are a lot of men who would like to see these women go away." He referred to a quote hanging over his wife's desk that reads: "Whatever women do, they must do twice as well as men to be thought of as half as good." He added, "There's still an old boy network out there, no matter how much progress there has been. But there is a growing, begrudging respect for women among their male counterparts." He added, "There's no malice involved. There are just men who don't get it. They really don't get it."

When I asked a male executive producer in Washington what he's observed over the years, he said, "I realized I was sexist when I had to tell my secretary to go on the set to tell the female anchor that it was too cold in the studio to go braless."

He said he constantly receives resumes from aspiring on-camera female journalists. He views the question of physical appearance as more one of avoiding distractions on the screen rather than seeking beauty. That philosophy was behind his decision to ask the anchor to don a bra. "I eliminate the women who are too attractive," he said, "and those who are hard to look at."

A famous female journalist who has commanded million-dollar contracts for her work said, "It isn't a matter of being beautiful. The question is 'can you communicate?'" But she admits she probably wouldn't be hired today to anchor a local station unless her reputation preceded her.

A female TV reporter for over 30 years feels that women, by and large, don't always get the best jobs. "They're not anchoring on the major network newscasts enough, and they don't have many of the top management jobs. Male executives hire with their gonads. They tend to go with the image of the grade-B blonde movie actresses they used to watch on TV when they were young."

Another added that, "So many women on TV are blonde because they represent to male executives the girl they couldn't date in high school."

Is the choosing of women for on-camera jobs as cynical as those comments would indicate? Hopefully not, but to some degree they do mirror the reality of television that has always been there and remains today. It's a visual medium in which physical appearance counts.

"Yes, we're in a cosmetics business," said a male network executive vice president in New York. "We're paid to win." Overall, he feels that women have been treated "quite well" in television. He said, "I am concerned about a lack of women in management. Most women who came into this business in the past wanted to be on the air, probably because of the pay-scale differences and the glamor. That is changing."

His concern is shared by many in the media who feel that there isn't enough female input into the major decisions that determine what stories are broadcast each day into millions of American homes. That situation will be resolved, hopefully sooner rather than later, through a combination of top male executives opening up the managerial ranks to women, and women who are willing to eschew the glamor (there really isn't much, believe me) of being on-camera and being recognized on the street and in restaurants.

In the meantime, TV newsrooms, which I see as a microcosm for women in most professions, are mostly still managed and controlled by men, and often their preconceived, deep-seated attitudes toward women come to the forefront. In some cases, it's well-meaning.

Diane Sawyer was in El Salvador when a skirmish broke out in the war zone. Those in charge of the CBS reporting team were reluctant to send her after the story because, as one of them put it, "It'll put the whole crew in jeopardy by sending a tall blonde woman." There was no time for Sawyer to change into fatigues and cover her hair, and a male correspondent went in instead. Actually, Sawyer was given the choice but elected to not place the crew in more danger than it already was. She understood the decision, but it is an example of a woman being treated differently than a man.

Fortunately, there are now many examples of women dangerously reporting from the frontlines. In fact, as WCI was working intently to get women out of Afghanistan, we relied heavily on brave female reporters like Clarissa Ward from CNN.

Everyone I interviewed had his or her own story of sex discrimination where assignments are concerned. Each, I suppose, reinforces the thesis that men view women in the newsroom, and in too many other professions, the way they were brought up to view them in general. That isn't inherently bad, but when it gets in the way of a woman's chances to cover major events on the same footing as a male colleague, it naturally raises hackles, especially for those of us who raised or are raising girls to be fierce competitors.

"No matter what you say or do," a female VP at ABC told me, "A woman still must deal with the natural relationship between men and women."

Will that "natural relationship" ever change to the extent, or in a way that will foster true equality in the workplace? Most people think it has, and it will continue. Some think it will happen as younger men enter management, men who've been raised in less traditional homes (like mine) where mothers worked and where gender roles were not as clearly defined and rigidly differentiated.

Some feel that being a woman in a male-dominated industry like TV can be an asset. One executive said, "When a woman interviews a top government official, he tends to think to himself, 'This is a piece of cake.' He assumes women are sweet and nice and won't be aggressive, don't have street-smarts, and says more than he might to a man."

But those instances are rare. The more common situation is for a woman to be assigned to conduct an interview with a man because the assumption was that the questions would be easier. Often, reality quickly set in as the interviewee was peppered with hard-hitting questions that left him bewildered and hopelessly unprepared.

And we haven't even broached the topic of non-binary and trans people, but I'll leave that to others more competent and experienced on the topic. Suffice it to say that I've seen my share of changes since I began my career and I've watched my children, and now even grandchildren, just beginning to find their way.

It's my hope that the industry will continue to grow and ultimately reach a state of equality, of fair representation to accurately portray our ever-changing world. Whether it's gender or race or orientation, there's room for everyone, especially in TV because it's a mirror of ourselves.

-❧-
FATHERS CAN BE MOTHERS, TOO

One time, my friend Janet came to Philadelphia to visit me, and she brought her daughter Sharon along. Sharon was twelve and a very progressive thinker. She heard us talking and heard me ask Janet about her mothering experiences. "Is this just about women?" she asked. "That wouldn't be fair. Fathers can be mothers, too."

Of course, she was right, then and now. There are a growing number of men choosing to be the parent who stays at home and cares for the children, maybe even working remotely. There are plenty of couples who share child-raising activities equally to allow each to pursue their careers.

Peter was a man who had chosen to stay at home and be the "house parent" as he called himself. "Soon after our last baby was born, we had three children, ages nine months, four years, and seven years, Ruth was offered a great job in media. She had done that type of work off and on for years and it was a great opportunity. I'm a graphic artist and decided that I could take this time to freelance. With Ruth's income, we thought we could make it work and give our children a good home life."

"Things can get hectic," he found. "I thought it would be a snap being a 'mother,' but I've found there are many things I didn't know. I can cook and do the laundry, but what do you do when you're talking to your client as one kid is about to conk the other with a baby bottle?"

He concluded, "It was more difficult than I thought at first, but soon it leveled out and we all found the right balance. One important thing I learned was the importance of not just entertaining them but nurturing them."

With the dramatic shift in family roles and dynamics brought on by necessity due to COVID-19, there has become a more equal distribution of household and child rearing responsibilities. That has served to demonstrate how resilient and flexible families can and must be to survive in our ever-changing world.

Caring certainly involves nurturing, and nurturing is often equated with physical care. It is much more. Nurturing children means being aware of their social, emotional, and intellectual needs as well as their physical ones. Fathers, as well as mothers, can nurture their children, but women often don't feel they can ask for help.

One evening we were getting ready to go on a family outing. I raced around checking six children to see if they were ready to go and that they were packing the proper items. When everyone was in the car, I felt disheveled and out of sorts. I looked at Ed. "It's not fair," I said. "Eight people have just left the house, and I was in charge of seven of them!"

"You're right," he said. "And I'd be glad to help, but you should have asked or told me what to do. You looked as though you had things under control."

I wasn't sure if I should be pissed or take it as a compliment. I had put myself into that role, and I repeated the action many times because that's basically how I was raised. I fell into my mother's pattern of running a household. I must admit, the next time we left the house in a gaggle, things improved considerably. But more to the point, it wasn't really anyone's fault. We were simply accepting a familiar pattern to bring order to the chaos.

Today's Wonder Woman is tomorrow's basket case. My advice to mothers is to be strong enough to break the cycle, even if it's easiest to just do it yourself. Sometimes, it's better in the long run to take a step back.

Even Wonder Woman needs a break once in a while.

One more story I remember vividly.

I was in Congress and on my way into the office with my assistant, Amy Sobel, when I said, "Let's drive by the cherry blossoms. They are in full bloom." Just as we did, I recognized my former coworker Willard Scott (who recently passed away) setting up for a remote weather shoot. I waved and he said, "Come do the weather with me! I'm on in 90 seconds!"

As I hurried over, I glanced to the side and saw the White House TV crew in a van. Then I saw Bill Clinton jogging with his friends. I hurried over to Willard. "Do you want me to see if Bill will help us out?"

"Absolutely!" He pointed to Bill and asked him to hold his position for a second and then he went live on the air for *The Today Show*. "This is Marjorie Margolies-Mezvinsky who as you may know used to be on the air with me and is now in Congress!" I smiled. "And look who's over here. Mr. President, could you help us with the weather?"

It was hard to believe all of that happened in under two minutes, but it was TV gold. Years later, anytime Willard Scott was in the news, this clip is included.

Only in Washington.

CHAPTER 12

A Deep Dive into Parenting

Any woman who understands the problems of running a home will be nearer to understanding the problems of running a country.

– MARGARET THATCHER

DURING MY TIME AS A HANDS-ON PARENT and working mother, there is no denying with so many children I probably encountered practically every situation a parent will come across. I learned so much about myself and the individuality of each of my children. Like all of us, I learned along the way and have found that those lessons still resonate today. As my children are now raising my grandchildren, they are running into many of the same situations, albeit with less children, but no less challenging.

I don't want you to think I was completely delusional in our crazy household, but one goal that I set for myself during that time was to try and make every day a thoughtful one for my children. Just writing that sounds silly, but that's what I did. There was so much going on in so many directions that I decided to try and meet that one goal for each child, each day. It was something I could work toward, something intangible yet important, in my opinion.

When I told my idea to my therapist friend, he told me that he felt the way a day ends for children often influences their overall attitude toward life. If they were put to bed happy—maybe with a story, a hug, and some individual attention—over time it may influence their overall attitude toward life. If they were just sent to bed, they were more likely to skew pessimistic.

"Children see life a day at a time," he said. "If they are just sent to bed, their day will end on a note of abandonment, misery, and loneliness. Children should go to bed with a feeling of satisfaction. Let me give you an example.

"One of my patients is a very successful businessman, but he's always worried that he will fail. He makes a great deal of money, but he's always worried it will vanish or the bank will fail. He feels that if he doesn't work extra hard, his success will only be temporary. When we explored his childhood, he told me that his father had vanished from the home and his mother reacted to that by constantly displaying anger. We'll call him 'Joe.'

"He could never remember his mother hugging or kissing him. He actually dreaded bedtime. She screamed at him almost every night, 'Go to your room! Don't wet the bed!' Many times, she even swatted him as he walked by.

"If your individual days end on a sour note," the doctor said, "so may all the tasks you undertake in life. If your days end on a happy note, it encourages you to look at life in an upbeat manner. How many times have you heard this? 'A couple should never leave an argument unresolved and go to sleep angry.' Giving your child a happy close to their day is an extension of the same theme."

Marie, a woman I met at social events, adopted a daughter named Bonnie when she was four years old. When Bonnie did something wrong, she would go to Marie and wait for punishment. "The first few times it happened, I burst into tears," said

Marie. "What kind of days did that child remember from her past? I spent the first two years of her life trying to give her happy days."

Giving your children a good experience doesn't mean giving them everything they ask for. That's taking the easy way, and it creates entitled kids. That's often the result of uninterested or distracted parents who'd rather pacify than exert the effort to share themselves with their children.

I was always amazed when even the smallest gestures make children happy. Once day, Susan came to my house to discuss some business. Marc wanted our attention and began to cry. Susan looked up. "Marc, if you let Mommy and me have some time together, I'll take you for a ride in my 'Jeep truck' when we are done."

"Mommy, too?" he asked.

"Yes, Mommy, too."

Another friend came to visit and brought Marc three fire engines because she saw how unhappy he was when I had accidently broken his. I gave him one of the trucks and saved the others to dole out when the opportunity arose. Only a few days later, Marc wanted to play with the car Vu was playing with. I couldn't convince him he had plenty of his own. So, I turned to a "new" toy, one of the saved fire trucks, and it worked.

Little children love the smallest things because it's the event, the act of giving, that gives them joy. I found that old boxes, tires in the yard, even empty makeup cases were treasures to my children.

It's often really easy to say yes to your child and hard to say no. When my children started to cry after I'd forbidden them something, I felt momentary twinges of guilt. But then I'd remember that my actions were done for their welfare. Mothers show they care when they say no and take the time to explain their decision.

A pediatrician told me that the childhood years should be peaceful, structured, relaxing, disciplined, challenging, and enjoyable. At first, I wondered how a household like ours with its constantly changing cast of characters and their daily schedules could include all those things. A peaceful life brings to mind stability. That didn't seem possible when I had to leave for work on a Sunday night right at dinner time, or Ed had to meet a client when one or more of the children had to be in different places at the same time. But that's not what peacefulness is. It's an inner feeling of calmness that is given to children and makes them feel secure. Peacefulness was also those times that I sat with one of my children without an activity or agenda, just being together. Often that's more powerful and meaningful than words.

Structure takes planning, and it was absolutely necessary for my family; however, that doesn't mean we had a rigid schedule that didn't allow for change. Structure is the pattern of the hours in our day. Bedtimes, mealtimes, work and school schedules formed the basis of our structure. Later, we had others living with us who were willing to help out.

There was a young woman named Liz who acted as our "rent-a-parent." At the beginning of every week, we sat down and tried to map out a schedule—that is, which child should be where at what time, what groceries were needed and when, what cleaning needed to be done, and on and on. It didn't always work seamlessly, but it was our attempt at juggling an exceptionally full household with each of our demanding careers.

Despite our best efforts at reducing work interruptions at home, for me there were always times that someone called with a news tip or breaking story that demanded my presence immediately. Such events disrupted our balancing act and caused us to reassess those carefully orchestrated weekly schedules.

Family life brings tension. There's no doubt about that. So that means setting aside time for relaxation. It sounds like a far-fetched dream at the time, I know, but it's essential. If I didn't add that "mommy time" to the schedule, I soon felt the tightening of the muscles in my back and neck. Sometimes, I could tell one of the children was stressed by their reluctant hugs. That was our bodies telling us to slow down and examine what was bothering us. I didn't always listen to my body then as I do now, but when I did, it was always more beneficial than I'd remembered.

Holly had severe allergies. In fact, she had nose bleeds that were so intense she had to be hospitalized for transfusions and have her sinuses reconstructed. Then she received regular allergy shots, which caused her to become tense with each injection. She and I talked about what was going to happen and how the anticipation is almost always worse than the actual event. Then we went to see Dr. "Ted" (Ted Tapper, newscaster Jake Tapper's father), and he talked to both of us and that seemed to help her. He was the right doctor for our family because he was not only kind but patient, and that's exactly what Holly needed.

For me, it was important to remember that a disciplined life, doing things we didn't always want to do, was a way to show my children that they had responsibilities based on their age and abilities. When Marc was three, I didn't expect him to keep his room clean, but as he got older I certainly did. That doesn't mean it wasn't a struggle because it was, but it had to be done. Lee Heh and Holly had to care for their rooms as well.

In some countries it is considered a privilege for children to help their parents. When parents wanted to punish a child, they told the child that he or she couldn't help out that day. Can you imagine that scenario? I pictured it in my mind many times.

Challenges are present every day in our lives. From learning to feed themselves to choosing careers, children face their own challenges. As a mother, I tried not to let my children struggle when there was no chance of their succeeding. There was one instance when I was writing a story, it was my wedding anniversary, we were packing to move to a new house, Marc needed attention, Lee Heh asked for help with her homework, my parents were coming by for a drink, we had an event to attend later that evening, and Holly had just gotten sick. I'm not exaggerating. That was the scenario, and I remember it vividly because it was one of the few times when I wasn't sure I could take one more thing, so I just said STOP. Let's prioritize, get the kids situated, and move some things around.

Enjoyment is doing things that are fun or making them as pleasant as possible. I had a neighbor who made a game out of clearing the table and doing the dishes. Each of her four children was assigned a role that began when dinner was over. She used her watch and called "Time!" That was their signal to complete their tasks. Of course, being children, they giggled and scrambled to avoid colliding with each other. She didn't even worry about their dropping something, because invariably that would happen. Her priority was establishing a routine of responsibility. Finessing the execution could come later.

Because of my job as a reporter and a member of Congress, my children got to do and see things that others probably didn't, especially in the time before the internet and social media. I took as many of them with me as I could if there was something like the arrival of a new panda at the Washington Zoo. It was a way for me to integrate them into my career just a bit. That gave us some much-needed time together and showed them that Mommy had a job to do.

By Morning's Early Light

When the alarms went off at our house in the morning, it was a signal for instant activity! During the summer, the pace was slightly less frenetic, but for most of the year, it meant the children were off to school, Ed to work, and I reviewed the story assignments I had. I found, once again, that organization was an important component in making things go as smoothly as possible and fulfill my mission of everyone beginning his or her day in a good mood. Some days, that was little more than a fantasy.

I talked to Ginny who had ten people, nine of whom were leaving the house within a half hour period of time. "How do you do it?" I asked.

"By having a lot of bathrooms," she laughed. "Actually, I encourage everyone to get as much done the night before as possible. Clothes out, lunches packed, books ready."

"I'm glad you said 'encourage,'" I said. "Wouldn't it be great if we all did that? Sometimes I don't, and then I grump at myself. I can be as lax as the children," I admitted.

Some mothers do these things for their children, but I always thought that learning to prepare is one step in developing responsibility. It's hard not to step in and do, but I try. Young children can pack their lunches just as well as mothers can (for the most part). That also helps teach cooperation, another necessary ingredient of family and adult life.

There were mornings when everything seemed to go wrong, despite my efforts to the contrary. But the next day when the alarm went off, it was a chance to start fresh. I tried to forget the previous day and put forth an effort to make the next one better. I found that children's memories were short, and they didn't generally hold grudges, which of course is a complete waste of energy anyway.

Another thing I told myself when the morning started off on the wrong foot was that there was no reason to assume the rest of the day would follow suit. I called that tactic "keep hoping."

Probably the hardest thing to deal with in the morning was the play all the children tried. I called it "delay tactics." Those tactics could also be used effectively at other times during the day. Sometimes they could be pleasant. "Just one more kiss, Mommy." "Let me hug you one more time." Other times, they were not. Just when I was ready to lock up the house, one of them would sit down on the floor and declare, "I'm not going."

Marsha, a good friend, told me she replied to that behavior with, "Well, I am." She'd go out the door, and invariably the reluctant child would follow. Every mother has to develop her own tactics to survive those dallying children. She has to have her own way to try getting them off to school so that she can begin her own day.

When Everyone Wants to Talk

There were evenings when I came home from work in an acute state of exhaustion to find one or all of the children had something they just had to tell me, and it had to be right then. It was difficult to concentrate and give each of them attention when all I wanted to do was go to bed. I wanted to say, "Can't it wait until I can think straight?" Most times, I tried to put my exhaustion aside, at least temporarily, and concentrate. Holly had a distinct talent for finding those moments with me.

"Mom, I need five allowances so I can go skiing," she said one day.

"Holly, I'm tired. Let's talk about it later."

"I have to let Susie know right away."

Before I could answer, I had to think about what her behavior had been, our plans, the budget we'd set. Trying to be calm and rational can be a challenge when your children are, well, challenging you.

The child therapist I talked to said he once had a patient who didn't say a word for her first two sessions. Not a word. He filled in the silence with talk of how the therapy process worked. When she began the third session the same way, he suggested that maybe she was wasting her time and money on therapy with him. She looked at him and said, "I have four children under seven at home. It's so nice not to have to talk or even listen if I don't want to. I just enjoy the silence. Sometimes I feel trapped. It seems as though the kids are always having a crisis at the same time. It's gotten so I just stand up and scream, 'SHUT UP!'" She began to sob. "I don't want to be that kind of mother. I want my kids to be happy."

"What kind of mother?" the doctor asked.

"A bad mother."

"I don't think you are. What you need is to learn how to set priorities. When all your children start talking at once, ask yourself if the subject is life-threatening. Obviously, you wouldn't scream at two children who are physically fighting. Then ask if it is necessary to answer more than one question at a time. You might try to give each of them a special appointment time to meet with you and talk about other things. It will make them feel important to have a special time with you."

Scheduling time with your children for an alone/together time may seem strange, but for many mothers, that may be the answer to developing a new and different relationship with their children. The case is usually many children sharing one mother, and everyone wants a piece of her time. When they all want the same thing, it can be frustrating.

Brenda, an acquaintance of mine and a writer, keeps her study door open. Her children are free to pop in at any time. Her only rule was that they sit quietly until she looked up, unless of course it was an emergency. This approach worked for her because she is able to work remotely. For many families, it's also become an issue because of the pandemic.

Susan's children all came home from school at different times. Susan didn't have a job (aside from being a mother and wife) so her afternoons were free. She waited in the kitchen for her kids to come home, and each one had about fifteen minutes of her undivided time before the next child arrived. She felt the schedule gave her time to hear what happened that day without interruption and to identify anything that should be discussed later. She was fortunate; time is not usually so conveniently divided.

Snatching a few minutes alone with each child is important for you and the child. But let's be realistic: it's not always possible. My method of finding time was to try and leave early for appointments or take the long way home when I was with one of the children. Another way to sneak in some quality time was to just pop into their room as they were getting ready for bed. By that time, quiet had settled throughout the house and that made the time feel even more special. When the girls were quite young, they had different bedtimes because of the gap in age. That allowed me time to focus on them individually. Once I added that into our daily routine, it was relatively easy to follow.

On Holly's first day of camp, I arrived to pick her up and noticed she looked a bit glum. "What's wrong?" I asked her.

"I don't think they like me," she said softly.

That one statement told me it was the perfect time to take the long way home. Her remark had struck a chord with me. I had attended my high school class reunion, and someone walked up to me and said, "You never had to worry about being popular." That was strange to hear because I certainly had. I shared that story with Holly during our drive and told her how I worried about being liked in school. Then I shared how at the reunion I found out some people had a completely different opinion of me than what I imagined they thought. I was too much in my head, and I think Holly could get that way as well. We had a good talk about what it meant to be afraid of what others think and how that is almost always wasted energy.

Another evening, Marc gave me a different kind of experience. We were alone in the car when he pointed to the moon, which wasn't full at the time. "Mommy, Mommy," he said, "moon broken!" I giggled and talked to him about the phases of the moon and how we can see it differently depending on the time of year. A beautiful stolen moment together.

I actually enjoyed the times I'd end up alone in the car with one of the kids. It gave us one-on-one time to share with each other outside of the household commotion. During one such ride, Marc asked me if there really is a God. I carefully explained to him that there are many theories on the subject and people around the world have different beliefs. He was silent for a moment and then said, "So I go to Sunday School every week and there's a chance that there's no God? Even God wouldn't think that was fair!"

Family Fun?

For us, family outings could be fun, or they could be a disaster. Most mothers have experienced something similar. We put all this time and energy into planning for a great trip, and it doesn't always go to plan. With so many personalities in our house, I learned that our attitude as parents often helped set the mood.

I know a family with two boys who often talk about the adventures that their mother took them on when they were little. I asked Grace, the mother, to tell me more about those wonderful trips.

"Just take one of our first outdoor adventures as an example," she said. "I was taking the boys to a nice local lake for some fishing. I thought I knew where I was going (since there was no GPS), but my sense of direction isn't the greatest. The lake was only fifteen minutes from our home, but after an hour of aimless wandering, I knew I was lost. Tommy looked at me and asked, 'Where are we, Mom?' I smiled and said, 'Don't worry. We should be there soon.' What they didn't realize was that I had to circle back to our house and start all over.

"That evening, all the boys talked about was the 'exploring trip' that I had taken them on. That was the first of many such events, and it was never planned but just a result of my inability to follow instructions. What may be seen as a fault turned out to yield the most memorable trips of their childhood. A calm, relaxed attitude was key."

Calmness is a beneficial quality for a mother to cultivate when taking children on trips. Patience is another. It can be difficult when you're on an outing with more than one child and each of them wants to go in different directions, or one dawdles while the other wants to run.

Then there's the time a child may throw a tantrum in the Museum of Natural History. Museums are built to amplify sounds. That happened to my friend, Lois. She said it was very difficult to stay calm and patient when people were looking at her as though she were abusing her child.

My girlfriend Janet said, "I remember one day when little Keith sorely tried my patience. I had taken him to the Fort Worth Children's Museum, which is a fantastic place. After that, we were going to lunch at his friend's house. I had been told to plan at least two hours for the museum visit. Keith went through the entire place in half an hour muttering, 'I've seen it. I've seen it.'

"When we were outside, I asked him what was wrong with the museum. 'Nothing,' he said. 'We can come back some other time so I can play with the things in there. I want to get to Bobby's so I can have a lot of time to play at his house.' I shook my head. I'd placed more emphasis on the museum while his focus was elsewhere."

Having a good sense of timing when planning family outings can be important, especially as your children reach the teen years. It's one thing to pick up on the spur of the moment when your children are small, but as they get older, your spontaneous decisions may conflict with their plans or changing moods. You may also be selecting an outing that is not of interest to them during that evolutionary period in their lives.

A therapist told me about a family session he once conducted. The mother of four teenagers complained that the children didn't want to go anywhere as a family anymore. Sometimes not wanting to travel as a group can be a sign of rebellion. Other times it can mean that what has been planned is not of interest to them anymore. I had to remind myself that just because they'd enjoyed an activity in the past didn't mean they still had those same interests.

A coworker named Stephanie told me how she tried to convince her fourteen-year-old son that being with the family was going to be fun. All he continued to say was, "I don't feel good. I want to stay home." She told him he wasn't being fair to the rest of the family and that everyone had been looking forward to it for over a week. She told him, "I suppose that little gang you run with has come up with something better to do than spend time with your family." She said she felt guilty when she discovered he had a 101-degree temperature.

In my experience, for a family outing to succeed, is has to be a group project from beginning to end. The children have to provide input on where to go and what to do. That doesn't mean they have control, but they will feel good about sharing their ideas, which might turn out to be worth considering.

We had an especially meaningful vacation on Margarita Island in Venezuela in the late 1980s. Seven or eight of the kids had come along on the trip (if we're counting). It was one of those magical times when everyone was enjoying the camaraderie and appreciating all that we were able to experience. The boys were hanging on Holly's every inappropriate word, and things just seemed easy.

It was one of those family moments that was so special because it was so unremarkable.

Positive Discipline

There's no getting around the fact that discipline is a necessity. Children often do things that are not only wrong but can even be harmful to themselves or others. Small children fight over toys. Some adventurous youngsters will go swimming where they shouldn't. Teenagers will try to bend or even break the rules if they feel they can get away with it. As a mother (and now a grandmother), I always tried to make "corrections" as positive as I could. Many people told me that if you tell someone often enough that they are bad or troublesome, the resulting energy will manifest into the child acting out.

The therapist told me that he interviewed an adolescent boy who had been caught shoplifting numerous times. The boy said that he'd had an aunt who always told him that he was "trouble" and that he would end up in jail one day. She had called him a thief when he took food to his room. For some reason, his mother never intervened. As a result, the boy lived up to his aunt's predictions.

Discipline means there has to be rules. I wasn't a fan of making a lot of rules for my children because I thought it would be oppressive for them. And even for the rules I did make, I tried not to enforce them by communicating with words like "you can't" or "you won't." For my kids, I felt that would be too unyielding and allow no room for mistakes. I always saw rules as guidelines, not rigid commands. I was always sure that if I made something forbidden, it would not end well. I knew that from my own childhood.

My parents seldom had "junk food" in the house. When I went away to college, my biggest vice was pigging out on any sweets I could put my hands on. I became an Oreo freak! Gaining weight during the first year of school (the "freshman 15") was all too real for me.

One day, Lee Heh and I were doing a radio talk show about rules and discipline. A caller asked her, "Does your mother tell you absolutely yes or no?"

"Rarely," Lee Heh answered. "She usually says it's up to me."

"Oh," the caller responded. "You really should have rules to follow, you poor thing."

"My mother has rules. She just doesn't make anything forbidden. She doesn't tell me I absolutely can or can't do something because that would make it more tempting, and I'd want to do what I was told I couldn't. Usually, she gives her opinion on why she thinks I should or shouldn't do something, but ultimately, it's my decision. I usually take her advice."

I was proud of her and so pleased that she had understood what I had been doing. Those interviews were always so interesting and enlightening because I heard things that we hadn't discussed specifically.

I was talking with my friend Diane about discipline. "You're right about forbidden fruit," she said to me. "For me, yelling is the worst thing a mother can do. I learned about that when I overheard Molly playing with her dolls. 'I don't want you to ever do that again,' she screamed. 'You could have been hurt playing near the road. Also, you need to pick up your toys. You cannot clutter up this house.'

"Then I wondered, do I sound like that? Of course, I had to admit to myself that I did. My voice and tone were conveying the message more harshly than I'd realized. After that eye-opener, I worked hard to tweak my parenting style."

With discipline, there is no win/lose situation. Discipline should not be used to show your children that you are stronger, that you can restrain them or that you are always right. It should be used to help them be better versions of themselves, usually without their realizing it. Sometimes you may even have to establish intermediate steps toward a goal.

Susan used that method effectively. Her youngest daughter, Tamara, went through a phase during which she wouldn't keep her room clean. Susan first told her if she would put her dirty clothes in a basket in her room for a week, she would get a reward. When Tamara managed to follow the instructions, she was rewarded. Then Susan added another step toward a clean room and a slightly more valuable reward. She continued this method until the final goal was reached. Tamara had kept her room clean, and she no longer needed the small rewards.

I remember when Holly began reading Judy Blume's book *Forever* long before I thought she was ready for the experience. When I told her that I didn't feel she was old enough, a battle began.

"You can't tell me what I can read," said Holly.

"Technically, you're right," I said. "You have your own life. I can't stop you from reading that book, and I'm glad you told me about it. I know you can read it under the covers with a flashlight. I hope you'll listen to me when I say that I think something is not quite right for you. That's what I think about this book at your age. It would be less time-consuming and easier for me to say 'yes, go ahead.' But I want to be honest with you about my thoughts because I care about you. If I didn't, I wouldn't even bother."

"Are you mad at me?" she asked.

"I'm not angry with you, and I don't think you're a bad person just because you want to read a book that's too old for you."

She was silent for a moment. "You're right, Mom. I won't read the book now. I didn't think about it like that. I actually agree with you. It's a bit grown up."

Now, who knows if she read the book without my knowledge, but that wasn't the point. I wanted her to understand that the decision was hers, but there was no reason she couldn't wait and do it later, when she was ready.

I always found that caring is the crux of discipline. When a mother cares, she tries to make disciplinary situations into positive encounters between her child and herself.

Say Goodnight

Bedtime could be a bright ending to a long day, or it could be a vast darkness. I noticed when my children were overtired, bedtime could be an unhappy time for them...and me.

The therapist told me about a woman who hated to go to bed. She came to see him because she had become addicted to sleeping pills, and she wanted to break the habit. "Why are you afraid to sleep?" he asked her.

"I don't know."

"Tell me about your bedtimes when you were a child."

The woman was silent for a moment. Then she began to cry. "My mother spanked me almost every night so I wouldn't dream about doing bad things when I was sleeping."

"What happened then?"

"I was angry and sad," she said. "I used to lie awake because I was afraid that I would dream about bad things. I guess my sleep troubles started back then."

Many mothers make bedtime more enjoyable by reading a story or following another routine, talking about the day or something the child can look forward to. These rituals often continue long past the time when their children can read or need so much reassurance before bed. They become accustomed to the routine and like how it makes them feel.

In our family, when Marc and Andrew were young, we had a nighttime ritual called "covers." Ed and I committed to rubbing their backs at least 100 times to help them fall asleep. Then we add their age to the count for a few extra rubs. So, if I was rubbing Andrew's back and stopped at 100, he'd say, "I'm seven so I get seven more rubs." It worked wonders for us and gave us quiet time with the boys.

Recently, I talked to one of my children who now carries on the "covers" tradition with his children. Janet told me that she always kissed her children, and then said, "Night, night, see you in the morning. I love you." Sometimes her boys would say the same thing to her when they got older, and she was going to bed first.

I tried to always say goodnight to each child with a kiss. Even when I arrived home after they were already in bed, I still snuck into their room to complete the ritual. Usually, they weren't aware of my intrusion, but sometimes Holly especially would roll over and say, "Huh? What?" Then she'd fall back to sleep.

I used to say, "I'll see you in the morning, too." Sometimes a story that I covered had a deep effect on me and my mothering style. When I was covering the Viscidi funeral, another tombstone caught my eye. Engraved into the granite was a rabbit, a kitten, and the words, "See you in the morning." While I was riding back to the newsroom, I could barely see my script because I was thinking about how much those words must have meant to that child.

Talking with Your Children

There are all kinds of shibboleths that give views about communication.

"The pen is mightier than the sword."

"Talk is cheap."

"Sticks and stones can break my bones, but words will never hurt me."

As a news reporter, I knew the value of the right word at the right time, and always tried to find the right questions to ask. As a television reporter, I also understood that communication has many levels. There are of course, the choices of words and vocal tone, but gestures, body stances and facial expressions, may be just as important. When you are communicating with your children, your physical size in comparison to theirs is something that most of us tend to forget about. My friend Stacey expressed this rather well. "There was a big change in the way we talked to each other when I suddenly discovered I had to look up to my oldest son."

Your stature and raised voice combined can sound mighty forceful to a toddler. Sometimes that may be the intent, but most experts I spoke with agree that a normal voice to a child in a normal situation is enough. A slight shift is noticed by children, and that usually conveys the message with enough impact.

There were times when I thought the word that I used the most was "no." And remember, my style was to not issue ultimatums, but I still found myself having to say no quite often. Especially when they were younger, that word was really the quickest way to stop an unwanted behavior.

I came home one night after my commute from Washington to Philadelphia. The next day, we were taping some family commercials for Ed's political campaign. I had rented all kinds of equipment that was scattered around the living room floor. All the children were there...ALL of them! Then there was the camera crew planning the shoot. I walked in and it was inevitable. "Mom, can you look at this?" "I need to ask you something important." "Do I have to go to school tomorrow?"

It was an ambush pure and simple. Marc was little at the time and surprisingly quiet. He pointed at his nose several times. Finally, I asked, "Do you have something in your nose?"

"Jess," he said.

"Yes? Okay, did you put it there?"

"Jess."

I looked at his nose and saw there was a small piece of metal lodged inside. I tried to get it out, but it kept going in farther. I quickly ushered him into the car and went to the emergency room. Marc wasn't terribly cooperative. The resident doctor on call could not get it out. Neither could the ENT specialist who was called in. They said Marc would have to be admitted, and they would put him under general anesthesia. What was I going to do with all those people at my house? The equipment, the crew? Plus, Marc and I were supposed to be in the commercial!

But most important, I knew it was just a little something in his nose and didn't like the idea of putting him under at such a young age. "Please try again," I pleaded. Someone found a suction tube that was able to remove the device. It was a clip used to attach gloves to a winter coat.

"Jess," Marc said when he saw it. "Marc put that in his nose, Mommy."

Words are a very important part of communication and a child's vocabulary grows rapidly. Sometimes their understanding of the meanings of words doesn't keep up with their vocabulary. Many times, you think your child understands a word only to find there was a misunderstanding. Other times, you may feel that you can use a grownup word in your child's presence only to find out your child clearly understands the meaning. Words figured prominently in my profession, so there were many times when I had to run to the dictionary or Thesaurus for help.

Martha told me her son, Billy, knew when she was angry, and his response was to disappear. She asked him how he knew because she rarely lost her temper or even raised her voice. "You say words more quietly," he said. "When you talk low and slow, I leave. I know when it's safe to come back because you talk normal again."

Actors are quite adept at using vocal tones to evoke imagery and emotions. A sentence can be delivered in different ways depending on the intended meaning, just by altering the tone and delivery.

As I stopped for a red light one day, I saw a young girl run up to an older woman. "Hello, rat," called the woman. Her love for the girl rang out in her voice and the child's excited reaction followed suit. What could be considered an unflattering name didn't bother the child at all, partly because of the way it was delivered.

"Don't do that!" a mother shouted as she wagged her finger. That may be one of the most common gestures a mother uses with a child. There are many other mannerisms that have a similar connotation. Many people have gestures that are part of their personality, how they communicate. My friends and family can often understand my mood by the way I use my hands and body. I can pick up those clues in my children as well.

One psychiatrist told me about a mother/son therapy session in which he discovered how the mother was subtly showing her hostility to her ten-year-old son. Every time the boy spoke, or his name was mentioned, the mother physically tensed up. She was unable to admit that she had hostile feelings toward her child whose unexpected arrival had cut short her acting career. The doctor recorded the next session and played it for her. Once she saw herself, she was able to begin exploring her feelings toward her child and their relationship gradually began to improve.

A gesture is generally made with the hands, but often the whole body telegraphs a message. Many mothers pay attention to their children's body language. We can often tell when the children are happy, sad, or angry just by the way they stand or walk.

I could tell that Holly was going to have a difficult day because her entire body project defiance from the start. The way she sat, stood, and walked around the house let me know exactly what kind of mood she was in. In those instances, I prepared myself, and tried to keep that in mind when I interacted with her.

There was a contest at Holly's junior high school in which the students had to transform themselves into an actual bench. She and I worked together on how the skit would be performed and how she would "become" the bench. It was quite involved, and hilariously well-done. We got into a bit of an argument, but I brushed it off and couldn't wait to hear how she did in the show.

A few days later, I went to the school and the principal stopped me. "Where have you been?" he asked.

"What do you mean?" I responded, somewhat confused.

"The students put on the performance last night, and Holly won! I was sure you'd be there!"

She was angry with me and that's how she decided to punish me. We'd worked on that together, and she knew how invested I was in the outcome, so she withheld the information from me. It was her way of making a point.

Joan told me a story about her family. Her daughter, Ella, was at a school for children with behavioral problems. Ella was at home for a day visit to see her father. Joan had worked that day and came home exhausted. When it was time for Ella to return to school, she asked Joan to take her. "I'm too tired to drive," Joan said. "I'm so tired I don't think I can do it."

"That's okay," Ella said.

Joan looked up and saw that while her daughter's voice was calm, her face certainly wasn't. "Ella, your face says you're angry with me, and I think you're not being fair. This visit was arranged so you could see your dad. You know I worked all day, and you can see I'm tired. I didn't even eat dinner. I know you want to spend time with me, but his visit had a different purpose. I hope you can think about that, and even talk to your therapist about why you feel this way.

"You know, I actually felt intimidated by her look," Joan said to me. "Ella's in that school because she has acted out physically in the past. I can see when she's getting close to losing control."

To effectively communicate with children, some say it's best to put yourself on their level. At first, I thought that meant my choice of words had to be within their grasp, but one day, I realized that when I was physically at their height level, our communication was enhanced. It's a technique some restaurant employees use when they kneel down beside a customer's chair to take their order.

After that, I began having talks with the children while sitting down on the sofa or even on their bed. When they were quite small, I often held them while talking. It made us almost eye level with each other.

A nurse told me that she communicated with an abused child, who showed signs of being autistic, by sitting on the floor with him and rocking and grunting when he did it. Soon, he began to laugh at her and that led to better interaction between them.

The Twelve-Word Rule

While all your verbal communications with your children have meaning, not all of them start out with that purpose. A general conversation can turn into an educational experience for both you and your children. Other verbal interactions are direct responses to questions, and sometimes those questions can make you squirm, test your patience, or show you how much you don't know. There are times when my children's questions made me wonder how on earth I was going to answer them.

Children ask questions because they are trying to identify themselves and their relationship to the people and places around them. Those questions are based on their need to know.

One of Holly's teachers once asked me, "Does she have to ask all those questions?"

"Yes," I replied. "Holly has a real need to understand. Are they really that difficult?"

"Well, she often wants to know more than what is planned in the lesson."

I met with the principal who told me, "There are no teachers in this program who can really deal and communicate properly with Holly." I'd been trying to figure out what was going on and how to address Holly's learning needs within the structure of the class. One of the things I found out was that Holly was kept inside during recess because she had trouble learning how to spell the word "elephant."

The principal took the time during our meeting to help Holly with the word. He divided the word into easier sections and made jokes about the letters. In no time, Holly was able to spell it herself. She had the ability but needed to receive the information in a different way from most of the children.

He then suggested that we enroll her in private school where she could get similar attention that would help set her up for success. The next time we moved, we decided to put Holly in a private school, and she thrived in that environment.

I met Helen, a psychoanalyst who often held group sessions for patients, during one of the stories I was working on. Since that time, we have continued to connect, and she gave me some advice about my own children. She said to me, "Try to answer your children's questions in twelve words or less." I laughed but saw that she was serious.

"I don't think you mean that literally," I said.

"What do you think I mean?"

"I think you mean I should think before I answer and choose my words with care. I should be brief and to the point. Children don't want lectures. They want simple, concise answers."

Helen nodded. "Often when I tell parents this, they either think I mean they should count their words, or they think I'm being dogmatic. I tell them to think about their values and position, to plan what they're going to say, sometimes even before the issue arises. You can think about how you're going to tell your children about sex before they ask. Then when the right moment comes along, you'll know where you stand."

"Doesn't that seem a bit forced and artificial?" I wondered out loud.

She smiled. "If you do something often enough, it will become a spontaneous action. Some parents cling to this idea and try to apply it rigidly. Of course, you have to be flexible when dealing with children. I try to encourage parents to try this method before they reject it. You know, you can't truly judge something before you've tried it. If you've never eaten eggplant, how do you know you don't like it?"

While that rule seemed simplistic and easy, believe me, it was not. I know because I had a child like Holly with her eternal quest to know, well, everything. She always wanted more and would lead me into conversations that could go on for hours. Then she'd say, "I feel good, Mom. You always answer my questions." Then I learned that sometimes she used those questions to divert my attention.

One evening, we began talking about how much she'd improved in the past few years. She liked to hear stories about herself. "Do you realize what you were like five years ago?" I began a story. Suddenly, I realized we'd missed her bedtime.

"Can you tell me more stories?"

"No, it's time for bed." I'm sure she would have pushed until 2:00 in the morning if I had let her. My Holly was a triumph and a challenge. She kept me on my toes as a mother, no question about that.

When I tried to apply the twelve-word rule, I had to consider the situation, the child involved, and the type of information to communicate. My own knowledge and feelings about a subject in question were also important. It was when I wasn't sure how I felt, or when I wasn't prepared for a particular question that my answers tended to meander.

One evening, Lee Heh and I were sitting in the dining room when Holly joined us. "What does it feel like for you and Daddy to have sexual intercourse?" she asked.

"That's an interesting question," I replied, and wondered what she was getting at. I tried to decide how to respond. This was certainly not a question I was prepared for, at least not in such a direct manner.

"I knew you were going to say that," Holly said. "Mom, you're just stalling for time."

"You're very clever." I took a deep breath. "It's a warm feeling. But I think you're asking if it hurts." I looked at her face but couldn't decide if she wanted more or had enough. "Sometimes in the beginning, there's some discomfort, but it doesn't hurt. It's exciting and wonderful when you are making love with someone you are in love with. It's a way of sharing." She looked on. Then the telephone rang, and Holly ran to answer it.

Lee Heh looked up at me. "That was the rudest thing I have ever heard," she said. "I must admit I've thought about it, but I'd never have the nerve to ask you."

Later, Betty and I were talking about using the principle of twelve words or less. "It sounds great," she said, "but my kids never listen anyway. I talk and talk, and I get nothing in return."

"That may be the problem," I said.

Brevity in an answer to a child's questions can be best. I think that's why Helen told me about the twelve words. Twelve isn't the magic number. It's a guideline, a reminder to keep it short. A brief answer may provoke more questions, and that's fine, but at least you will know more about what your child wants to know and why. The answer many not even be as important as the question or your willingness to answer it.

Marlene has a son who was learning about roosters in school. One evening, he got in the bathtub with his younger sister. He began asking questions about the difference between his body and hers. Marlene tried to explain by referring to what he'd been learning in school. "Do you mean I'm going to grow up to be a rooster?" he asked.

Jennifer told me her girl Hanna was full of questions, and most began with "Mommy, why does..." She asked why the grass was green. Jennifer said, "She's only four. It took me two days to figure out how to explain chlorophyll to her. By that time, she had forgotten that she had even asked the question."

Not every question a child asks has great importance. Many times, his or her priority of the moment may have no importance five minutes or an hour later. Other questions will keep appearing with regularity, even when you feel you've already answered them. It helps to remember that children like repetition.

Children's attention spans are usually short. A particular question may be repeated until the child makes the knowledge their own. Another reason for the repetition is that questions asked may not really lead to what the child wants to know.

Right after his grandfather died, Sarah's son, Bobby, asked her many questions about death. Those questions weren't asked in one day but over a period of weeks.

"What does dead mean?"

"Do trees die?"

"How long will it be before Max (the dog) dies?"

Finally, Sarah asked, "Are you afraid you are going to die?"

"No," Bobby said.

"Are you afraid Mommy and Daddy are going to die?"

Bobby climbed up beside her and said, "Grandpop was your daddy."

Sarah had reached the basis of his questions. Now she could answer them in a concrete manner, keeping her answers short and simple, and well within his level of understanding.

Remembering + Sharing = Empathy

While I was interviewing the therapist, we touched on the problems of communicating with children. We talked about a number of ways to improve communications. Then he said, "I tell my patients who are having problems with their children that they have a lot to share from their pasts. By remembering their childhoods, and their feelings and reactions in similar situations, by sharing those experiences with their children, they can achieve empathetic understanding.

"A lot of them think they're doing this," he continued. "But their approach is, 'When I was your age, I would never have dreamed of doing that.' This puts the child on the defensive and also can equate a feeling that is something wrong with them."

Memories of the past are in part responsible for your approach to mothering. I have meaningful memories of the way my mother dealt with my sister and me. I also have memories of happy and sad events in my life. Those memories are not only of the events but of my feelings and emotions at the time as well.

Remembering can be a bridge over which you can travel to reach your children. You were a child and many of the frustrations your child experiences are similar to frustrations you experienced also. You thought your teachers were mean; your parents were unfair; you had fights with your friends; others called you names or made fun of you; you always wanted to be someone else. You can use those memories to help you as you care for your children.

When Holly first came to live with us, Lee Heh was hurt and upset by the amount of my time that Holly required. Our sharing and togetherness were limited by the new experience of having a sister. While trying to find a way to help Lee Heh understand, I thought back to my childhood and my relationship with my sister.

Phylis was ill when we were children. Often, I felt ignored and left out because of the amount of attention my mother gave her. My sister needed my mother's time more than I did, but that didn't stop my feelings.

"Lee Heh, I can understand how you feel," I said. "When I was a child, Aunt Phylis was sick. Nanny had to give her a lot of time. Sometimes, I felt angry and jealous because I needed my mother, too. You and I aren't the same, but we have feelings that are similar. Sometimes I wanted to push Phylis, but I didn't. I even wished she weren't there, but I always loved her."

Lee Heh nodded, and for a moment, we shared a togetherness and a closeness that can only be described by the word 'empathy.' We were able to become the other person if just for a few moments. That's what empathy is all about. It's not sympathy which is feeling sorry for the other person. Empathy is almost like seeing through the other person's eyes and feeling what they feel.

Remembering and sharing can equal empathy. It means walking for a fleeting moment in your children's shoes and trying to feel what they feel.

Those Challenging Questions

While many of the questions your child may ask you are of immediate interest, such as "Why can't I have a cookie?" or "Why can't I go outside?", there are other questions that will challenge you. The area that is your challenge may be the one which is the easiest for your best friend. Your answers to those sticky questions may depend on how well you know yourself in that particular area, and if you have sorted out your own views and values.

Helen told me that she tells the parents she treats to do their homework and prepare for those challenging questions before they arise. That means determining your own values about the major issues that will involve your children. In that way, a mother can help her child learn how to make judgments and progress to mature self-sufficiency. Your own values will probably be those of your children, with modifications due to individual natures. Children absorb values from their parents, other significant adults in their lives, and from their peers.

The three areas where I found the most challenging questions from my children were permissions, sex, and death.

Holly had a friend who had an influence over her that I didn't like. Because I didn't want to make anything "forbidden," I took time to think about what I should say when Holly wanted to go to that girl's house or to the mall with her. I could say, "No, you can't go. I'm your mother and I say no." That would be simple, but dogmatic, and it wouldn't help Holly learn to develop the necessary abilities to select as friends those people who were best for her. So, we talked about the friend and the amount of influence she had over Holly. We also talked about why I didn't want Holly to go to certain places with her. I didn't want to give an ultimatum but rather guide her into making a good decision for herself.

After I had presented a logical and truthful picture of my feelings and the reasoning behind those feelings, I had to hope that Holly would make the right choice. That's part of our job as parents, right? We give our best advice, set an example we want them to follow, and then send them out on their own.

Tammy is a friend who has one child of her own and four adopted children. Her bio-son is the oldest of the group. When the question of where babies come from arose in school, the teacher heard him tell the other children that they were wrong. "You get a catalog and then you pick the child that is best for you," he said. After being informed by the teacher, Tammy quickly explained to him that adopting was not the only way to have children. In fact, it wasn't even the most common way.

Lee Heh was always a private child, always wiser than her physical age would suggest. Sometimes, it felt like she was the adult, and being somewhat unconventional, I was the child. She would say, "Mom, you shouldn't put a sleeveless top on Marc. It's too chilly." She usually had a good point. Her maturity in some areas led me to believe she'd matured in all areas. I had to remind myself that it wasn't necessarily the case.

I wanted all the children to be prepared for intimate relationships, when the time was right, in such a way that the sexual experiences would not be negative or traumatic experiences.

So, I turned to the good doctor, my therapist friend. He told me a story about how a colleague of his had found a gynecologist for his fifteen-year-old daughter. "I'm not telling you when to call him and what you are going to do eventually, but I want you to have this number. If you are ever thinking about having sex, I want you to call him first."

I wasn't sure what to think about that. If I were that girl, I would have taken that as an endorsement. I would think if I had the number, perhaps I was ready. It was exactly the sort of thing I wanted to avoid with my girls. Of course, if I had suspected or was aware they were sexually active, I may have felt differently. I tried to deal with the topic as openly and honestly as I could. As parents, we must be realistic. If we face the facts, we will be less likely to be shocked. We must try to imprint our values on our children to combat the peer pressure that will inevitably come. The most important thing is that those lines of communication remain open.

I did a series of stories about family planning clinics and the thing that struck me was the number of frightened young girls who were there because they were afraid of their parents. Many girls I spoke with had never had any conversations with their parents about sex and birth control.

When my girls asked me about sex, I tried to answer them reasonably, putting emphasis on the caring aspects of a relationship. After all, sex is only one part of a loving relationship, although at that age it seems like the main part.

Holly asked me at one point, "How far do you think a sixth grader should go? Some of the kids in my class are going steady already. Kissing is first base, then second, third, and all the way. Some of them say they are at second and going to third."

"Holly, I have to be honest with you," I said. "Kids your age are just not ready. Sex is very important when you share it with someone you are ready for. I think the most important thing about sex is that you have to recognize when you are ready and when you aren't."

"When will I be ready?"

"I can't give you a specific age; no one can say that for sure. You really have to love someone and know they are the kind of person you want to get close to. Sex isn't something to be taken lightly. Your body is important, and it's your body. You can say no at any time. You know I've done stories about sexual abuse and children. Sometimes children are afraid to say no, especially to an adult. You don't have to be afraid to say no."

I never told them something that I didn't believe just to get them to behave in a certain way. When I gave advice or guidance, it was because that's what I felt was true. At WCI when we held the RAPP program in Kenya to help prevent teen pregnancy, what fascinated me was that the girls there didn't understand the concept of "consent." We spent a lot of time educating them on how to say "no." Most of them never realized that was an option.

Another area with challenging questions is death. That's where I found myself running into problems and responding with the easiest answers I could come up with. The toughest questions for me were ones like "Why did she die?" "What happens when a person is dead?" "Where do they go?" I'd often find myself using euphemisms and stumbling over words. With the topic of sex, I could answer from experience. Death was a different animal all together. I've seen people die, but until it happens to us, how much do we really know?

My friend Jean is a nurse who worked with dying patients for quite some time. Much of her work was done in the patient's home as part of their hospice care. I decided to talk to her because, being a reporter, my first instinct when confronted with a difficult question was to go to the experts.

"The first thing I'd say is not to frighten your children with the idea of death. I try to approach death as though it was a natural event in a life, and it is. Part of my philosophy is based on what I was taught as a child. My parents never used death as a threat or as a punishment hanging over my head. They also didn't involve religion in their discussion of death, even though both were quite spiritual. They always told me that death meant a person was no longer breathing, nor could they move or talk. They never said, 'It's sleeping forever.'

"As to where a dead person goes, they replied that they didn't know and that there were many theories. But I always remember that they said death was a natural event, and in some cases, it was best for the person who died.

"When my children were growing up, I used dead birds and insects to show and teach them about death. We often buried the dead creature and talked about death as it affected this bird or that bug. Then when my youngest, Leah, was four, I had a chance to see how effective my teaching had been. Her babysitter's husband died. Leah knew him and had been to their house often. When Sam was ill, she was able to understand and gear her playtime with him according to his physical abilities. Often, she just sat beside him in a lounge chair for hours.

"When he died, Leah seemed to understand what had

happened. Before we left for the funeral home, I tried to explain to her what she would see. Essentially, I told her that he was dead and that meant he was not breathing. I also told her she wouldn't be able to play with him and she could talk to him, but he wouldn't be able to answer.

"She looked at me. 'Is he like the bird the boys found and put in a box?'

"'Yes,' I said.

"'They digged a hole. Sam, too?' I nodded.

"When we reached the funeral home, she walked over to her babysitter. 'I love you,' she said. Then she walked over to the casket and stood on the kneeler. She touched Sam's hand and nodded. 'Bye, Sam,' she said and ran back to her babysitter. 'He doesn't hurt now. He did when he played games with me. That's good.' She climbed on the pew and added, 'You have the girls and everyone else...and me.'

"She showed the same kind of acceptance when her great-grandmother, both her grandfathers, and her great aunt died. There was always a feeling for the living and the ability to point to the future. She never reacted by becoming clingy or expressing fears about her mom and dad or herself dying."

"What would you have said if she had asked you where dead people go?" I asked.

"I'd say I don't know, because I don't," said Jean. "There's nothing wrong with saying to your children that you don't know if it's the truth. I say it a lot. Sometimes I even say, 'Let's see how we can find out.' I've never experienced death. Sometimes I think we attach too much mystery to the idea of death."

You may find the challenging questions for you are ones which are totally different than mine. If you know where you stand, you can answer your children in simple, clear language without making things a threat. In that way, you can help your child grow.

Fast Forward to Today

My children now have families of their own and I'd be remiss if I didn't provide their views on a few parenting topics from the Margolies-Mezvinsky home. They dutifully recalled several vignettes from the past, a patchwork of lessons many of them still find useful.

• **Disagreements** – Vu has taken many lessons and applied them to his own family. "When my two boys are having an argument, I remember lessons from my childhood and try to approach each situation with a sense of calmness. I learned from Marjorie not to overreact but instead to find the origin of the conflict and then work towards a resolution by using the logical brain, not the emotional brain. That comes from something Marjorie used to say when we were growing up, 'Before you fire, think, and only fire if necessary.' I think about that a lot and try to do that every day."

• **Equality** – Both Andrew and Vu remember countless situations where they were not only encouraged but expected to treat everyone with respect and kindness whether it was a political dignitary in our home or someone working in the service industry. That gave them the social skills and confidence to interact with people from all walks of life.

• **Mindfulness** – Several said they learned the importance of humility and kindness. One of them said, "I was very conscious of the fact that you rarely said a disparaging word about anyone, even if you were tempted to do so." With a career in politics, there were certainly many opportunities.

• **Status** - Regardless of our financial status at any given time, we sought to impart on our family a sense of self-awareness and frugality. So it was no surprise to me that several of them fondly recalled JoMar, the venerable thrift store that was somewhat ahead of its time. The stores were often located in transitional neighborhoods and their stock was everchanging. They would buy seconds and remainders from high-end stores and re-sell them for pennies on the dollar. Our family made an event out of our visits there, searching for bargains and even gimmicky clothes that were just fun to wear. Many of my children still talk about their favorite trips and the "finds" that they treasured for years.

• **Thinking Creatively** – With our focus on education and personal enrichment, we tried to instill a sense of curiosity and the ability to develop creative solutions to a problem. One of the boys remembers, "You guys taught me to understand the boundaries of 'the box' so that I could think outside of it."

Having my children apply some of those lessons to their own family is one of the most rewarding aspects of parenthood, watching them take what they learned and putting their own spin on it. But let me be clear. I often learned a lot from them as well, and still do.

In fact, one night I came home feeling out of sorts. Several years ago, I was running in a primary against another woman, something that didn't happen often back then. Before the debate, my opponent came over to me. I thought it was for some friendly banter, but the conversation was not pleasant. I always tried hard not to take "work stuff" home with me, but in that instance, I couldn't help it.

When I walked in the house, they knew something was amiss. I told them the story and said it was especially disappointing because it's tough enough for women without their being un-kind to each other. One of the kids looked at me and said, "Just consider the source, Mom."

I remember those wise words to this day.

CHAPTER 13

I Am F**king Learn-ed

*learned (two syllables) – adjective, describing a person who has learned
a lot about something. Wise, educated, otherwise smart.*

I LIKE TO SPLIT UP THE WORD "learned" into two syllables:
learn-ed. I've heard the usage is more common in the British
English although some claim it's archaic, relegated to areas like
law and stuffy universities. But I like it. I feel it represents what
I've been through, the things I've experienced, and the manner
in which I've acquired such knowledge, be it formal education
or diving into the trenches. (I mean that metaphorically, but
sometimes it *felt* literal.)

Through those experiences, I've amassed my share of knowledge about what worked for me, and possibly more importantly,
what didn't. Here are some lessons I've learned (only one syllable
with his usage) along that way.

~❀~

Don't Try to Be a Superhero

I learned so much from my parenting journey with the adoption of my first child. One important realization was that just because I'd initiated the process and gone into it on my own, I didn't need to prove anything. It wasn't necessary to do everything myself or try to impress others with my ability to juggle work and a child without breaking a sweat.

My journey was a bit of a public one because of the history-making circumstances, so I was prepared to be held to a certain standard, to prove that I'd made a wise decision, that I could be a good parent without having given birth to a child. The tables had turned because I found myself the subject of high-profile interviews, and this time I wasn't the one in control.

At first, I was under the illusion that I had to be perfect, that I had to show the world that as a single woman in the 1970s, I could do it all. I had to be the ideal representation of single parenting of an adoptee. Never mind that there have always been women (and men) who were single parenting for whatever reason. I was in the spotlight. The focus was on me.

And that spilled over into my personal life. I wasn't always able to be in control of situations where a child was involved. There was chaos and messiness and unpredictability. I'd understood that logically, but experiencing it shifted my life in a new, unexpected direction.

I eventually learned to welcome the unpredictability that came along with having an instant family. While Lee Heh was surprisingly adaptable with an easygoing disposition, I still faced the challenges that life throws at all of us, and I had to find my way.

At some point, I realized that doing it all and having it all were not necessarily the ideal, no matter how much the media tried to tell us otherwise. My thinking is that you can do it all, you just can't do it all at the same time.

The fact is that parents (single or married) do not have to be superheroes. We all have the same needs, the same fears, and the same concerns as everyone else. Everyone has his or her own circumstances, but that burden of pressure that we place on ourselves is not constructive or healthy. The superhero concept is simply a myth. Trying to do it all only results in extreme fatigue and inevitable frustration, and it makes you extremely cranky.

I hope that all parents understand that it's about balance. Having a support system is an incredible way to manage the load. My parents were initially apprehensive about my decision, but they ultimately embraced it and Lee Heh, as I knew they would. Their concerns were for my future and my well-being, and I realized and appreciated that. They wanted their child to have the best possible chance for a fulfilling life. But when they saw Lee Heh and welcomed her into their life, it felt like the most natural thing in the world.

The Holt Agency was another support system, as was the rest of my family and my friends. I wish I'd understood early on that I didn't have to be a superhero.

❖

I'd Love Your Help

When someone in your life, and especially your family, is easy to get along with and quick to please, it's wonderful and amazing. But some people aren't that way, and they are wonderful and amazing, too. There's no denying that it's a different experience, but that's one of the joys of being a mother: experiencing the variety of personalities, the different shades of love.

During my adoption journey, since the first one went so smoothly, I was unprepared for the challenges of the next one.

I had learned early on how to divide my time between work and family but dealing with a child who required more attention was a challenge.

Through it all—the drama, the tragedy, the struggles—there is real humor in life. I've learned to find that humor because it makes all the difference in the world when we realize we can smile. The most important thing is that we look back on tragedy and remember the humor. Staying positive is a conscious choice, and I choose that every day. Having such a large family, it was always important for me to make sure everyone felt included and important, whether they were a bio-child, a stepchild, an adopted child, or a visitor. It didn't matter. Those times of cama-raderie are what really mattered. It was about family. Still is.

That's when I learned to not only ask for help but to accept it when it's offered. Employ those three important words. I. Need. Help. As mothers, we are often taught, whether overtly or directly, that we must solve everyone's problems, that we are the fixers, that we should know instinctively how to handle any situation. Well, I'm here to tell you that is a myth. We aren't perfect and shouldn't be. Life and children and family are about learning and growing together. We learn from our experiences, both joyous and tragic.

Remember, these words are your friend: I Need Help.

⁓❀⁓

Guilt Is a Wasted Emotion

I've talked to the experts on child growth and development. Sometimes this occurred while I was gathering information for a story and other times, it was when I'd sought help in raising my own children. Not all these encounters with the professionals were in person on a one-to-one basis. I went through a period of time when I read every childcare book that came into my hands. I'm not sure I learned new things from these books, but they helped me crystallize my thoughts into new patterns. Sometimes I felt the books actually inhibited me. (I hope that's not what this book does for you.)

My friend Ronni Ginott is a former teacher and educational consultant. She's also the niece of famed child psychologist, Haim Ginott. She provided the following quotes that have been attributed to Haim.

"Happiness...is not a destination: it is a manner of traveling. Happiness is not an end in itself. It is a byproduct of working, playing, loving, and living."

"Children do not yearn for equal shares of love: They need to be loved uniquely, not uniformly. The emphasis is on quality, not equality. We."

"What is the goal of parenting? It's to help a child grow up to be a decent human being, a mensch, a person with compassion, commitment, and caring."

I can remember putting Haim's book down and thinking it was a masterful work. Then I tried to put his words into action. It took me awhile to relax enough to realize he did not expect me to master in a short period of time what he had devoted a lifetime to.

My mother and my close friends also helped me shape my ideas and feelings about what it is to be a mother. My mom was extraordinary, and so was my father. I was fortunate in that regard. They were over-protective in a very loving way. But most of all, my children helped me learn about mothering.

Since my journey into motherhood began many years ago, I have had time to clarify my philosophies. There aren't many so don't brace yourself for boredom. I've made them into an acronym which spells CHILD.

Caring. Mothers are for caring. I feel it's so very important for a mother to let her children know she cares about their daily experiences. Caring means a lot of things to me. It means listening, appreciating, explaining, saying no, and lots of hugs and kisses, or just a gentle touch. I like to think that the process of caring is the rock on which I built my style of mothering.

Honest. Honesty means being willing to admit you've made a mistake. This can be difficult, but it is important for children to see their mothers aren't perfect. Letting children see this helps them cope with their mistakes with more ease. Holly was good at catching my mistakes. She'd say, "You didn't mean that, Mom." And I'd reply. "You're right. I shouldn't have said that." Honesty means saying you don't know when you don't.

Informative. I've heard of mothers who make up information on subjects which they know nothing about just to give their child an answer. Then the child discovers his/her mother was wrong and stops trusting them. Being informative also means determining where you stand on many issues that may involve your children.

Learn-ed. That's my fourth philosophy. Children learn from observing the adults in their life and they often act the same way. Parents can learn from their children, too. I'm not the same person I was when I first became a mother. The same will happen to you if it hasn't already. My horizons have expanded and contracted at the same time. I was quite successful, but I don't think I ever reached the top of my journalism profession the way I once felt I would. My children meant too much for me to invest so much of my time getting there. Through my children, I'm still growing and learning. As each child entered my life, there were new skills to learn and a new person to care for. I am convinced the most selfish thing I've done (with regard to my own satisfaction) is to include children in my life.

Disciplined. That's the final word in my acronym. I never believed in physical punishment despite the fact that many in previous generations did. When I was doing a series of stories on child abuse, I learned that many of the abusing mothers (fathers, too) had been abused themselves as children. Physical punishment becomes emotionally hereditary, and it's destructive for future generations. The only thing physical punishment does is show a child this is the way adults act. They see this as acceptable behavior. There is no perfect way to be a mother. Your own way is best for you, just as mine was best for me.

Each child also has a different approach to the same stages of development than your other children. Being aware of your own individuality and that of your children is important to mothering.

What I learned is that discipline is not as much about correcting behavior as it is about being proactive, direct, explicit, organized, and communicative about what is expected.

At one time, there were thirteen people in my life who called me "Mommy." One of them was Mrs. Suu, the Vietnamese mother who lived with us. She was actually a few years older than I, but she heard the children call me "Mommy" and followed suit.

I answered.

⚜

You're Already Mother of the Year

In 1986, while we were in full family-expansion mode, I was bestowed with the Outstanding Mother of the Year Award. It was given to 10 mothers by the National Mother's Day Committee. I immediately felt like it belonged to my own mother as much or even more than it did to me.

I've incorporated some of these tips throughout this book, but here is the complete list of the 10 tips that I provided when I was given the Outstanding Mother of the Year Award.

1. Don't try to be super-mom.

2. Understand that you may not always get help—not even some of the time.

3. A clean room doth not a good person make.

4. A happy mother helps make a happy child.

5. Pick a husband with a well-developed sense of guilt.

6. Understand that the only way to avoid sibling rivalry is to have only one child.

7. Realize that once you're sure you've mastered one stage of childhood development, they're off to the next one.

8. Never, ever lose your sense of humor. In fact, develop and nurture it.

9. Respect your children.

10. Pick good parents.

Just remember, being named "Mother of the Year" and receiving that recognition is nice, but that attention fades quickly. As mothers, we don't need awards. We just need to do our best and set a good example for our children.

Raising them to be caring adults is its own reward...mostly!

⁂

Always Be Prepared to Lose

My approach to life has been nothing if not consistent. I was always toughest on myself because I liked to win. I enjoyed setting goals and achieving them. As they say, the journey is half the fun.

That's exactly the approach I took with my run for Congress and subsequent political efforts. And I've always been conscious of the fact that the children would learn so much either watching my journey or becoming involved, as they almost always did.

I never intentionally took on a challenge just to make a point or to show my kids that it could be done, but I made sure that they were as involved as possible and felt included. Depending on their ages, they may not have understood the importance at the time, but hopefully with maturity they would come to appreciate what I was working to accomplish despite all the challenges I faced and sacrifices I chose to make.

It was especially important for my girls to see that having a mother with a passion for adoption or a thriving career or a seat in Congress didn't have to be an anomaly. For them it was the only life they knew. What I hoped, and still hope, is that more and more girls see that they have options. Just because an occupation may have been male dominated in the past doesn't mean things can't change.

I certainly never saw myself as blazing a trail for women; that wasn't my motivation. It was simply that I found those professional challenges intriguing. I didn't seek them out because they were typically seen as a man's role, but I also didn't shy away from them because of that, either.

Maybe it's my optimism, but I've always seen an opportunity as a learning experience, a new challenge, and that's what inspires and motivates me. I'm not one to wait for possibility to present itself. I never approach a challenge with unshakable confidence, but I do have the ability to block out the negativity and naysayers. That helps me focus on the goal, and even when I was up against another job applicant or a political opponent, my concentration was never on them. It was always on my performance and what I knew I could do if given the chance.

As I've always said, "'You've got to be prepared to lose before you can win. You've got to get out of the stands and onto the playing field."

-~❦~-

Now's the Time

When I was in politics, I often visited schools in my district. I was speaking in an assembly at my son's school when a young girl raised her hand. "Who takes care of your children when you are not home?" she asked.

People knew that I had many children, so I ran into this question often and was surprised each time it happened. "Would you have asked that question to a male politician?" I responded.

The applause started from the female teachers and parents and traveled around the auditorium. Most of the young people had no idea why the adults were clapping and cheering. I tried to explain to the student that I was not trying to embarrass her, but especially as a female, she should understand that sometimes women are held to a different standard than men. Then I explained to her that I organized with my husband and older children to manage our atypical household.

Although I think things are changing, it bears repeating that as we age, men become venerable, and women become vulnerable. I remember when Barbara Walters confided in me, "You know when Dan Rather took over after Cronkite left, he was considered the young man on the block. Around the same time, I made a big move and was considered a grand dame who had *staying power*. Rather was a year older than me at the time."

That is why the UN Fourth World Conference on Women was so important to me and why I am passionate about WCI. We've been saying for years that things are changing, but it's up to us to keep that momentum going. We must educate upcoming generations and teach them than anything less than true equality is unacceptable.

It's important for us as women, and for our daughters and granddaughters.

―❀―

Six Qualities to Succeed

I'll keep this simple. Here's a list a friend shared with me years ago and I've remembered it. These are the qualities that can help one succeed in the world regardless of who they are.

1. Humor

2. A team player mentality

3. A can-do personality

4. A high energy level

5. Creative problem solving

6. Basic honesty

And, of course, a willingness to work hard for what you want...and deserve.

―❀―

Develop a Head for Numbers

According to the *2019 Report on the Economic Well-Being of US Households* conducted by the U.S. Bureau of Statistics, financial literacy varies based on gender. On average, women scored around 52% on financial literacy while men came in at 67%. This difference was attributed to the fact that statistically, women had less experience with financial decisions than men.

If I don't impart any other lessons, if you get nothing else from this book, every woman (or man) who is unaware of the family finances needs to make it her mission to become involved today. Not tomorrow, today. Sit down and talk about it. Don't let disinterest or not having a head for numbers stop you.

Trust me, I understand. It never fails that he will shove a stack of papers at you as you're heading to a dinner or an event and ask you to co-sign so they aren't late. It's tempting to just do it and go on to your fun event, but don't let that happen.

The other thing is to focus on your mental well-being and that of those around you. Be on the lookout for warning signs and address them immediately. If your suspicions turn out to be unfounded, all the better. You owe it to yourself to find out.

As mothers, we have to set an example for our children, especially our daughters when it comes to issues of money and power. Too many women take a backseat on household finances and setting a good example will show that both people need to be involved.

If you don't want to control the finances, at the very least, have scheduled meetings to discuss what's coming in, what's going out, and what the plans are for the future. I can't stress enough that this has to be every woman's priority.

⚜

Surviving the Unimaginable

Outliving a child is a scenario no parent wants to even think about, but it happens and it's part of our journey. Having the tools to deal with such a tragedy is key because as mothers, as parents, we have to keep going. We must do it for the rest of our family. It's up to us to hold everything together.

Holly was such a force of nature that those 48 years feel like a blur of energy and hilarity and mischief all rolled into one. God knows she was riddled with issues, but she had the other side as well, the joyous side, the adventurous side, the loving side, the hilariously inappropriate side. Not everyone got to see every facet of her, and I wish they had. Then they would see what I saw in her.

Here are a few suggestions to consider:

- Do give yourself time and permission to grieve, other things can wait.

- Do honor your child by allowing yourself to enjoy the good memories.

- Do communicate your needs to the rest of the family; let them know how you're doing.

- Do talk to others instead of keeping your feelings inside.

- Don't pressure yourself to recover quickly. Allow yourself to take all the time you need.

- Don't make any important decisions during such a difficult time.

- Don't shut out your support system; they want to help.

I can sum up this chapter as follows: You learn from the tough times, you learn from the disappointments, you learn from the rejections, you learn from the losses, and I am f**king learn-ed!

PART III

Reflections

I Have No Retirement Skills

WHILE OUR FAMILY seemed unusual at the time, we really weren't. That's because back then, there actually was no typical family and there still isn't. And that's a good thing. Our large brood was a visual representation of an evolving nation, the growing concept that family is much more than two parents and biological children. It's a collection of people who come together, through birth, adoption, sponsorship, or any other method. It's not the manner of arrival that's as important as the fact that they form bonds that hold them together forever.

Once, while looking at all our kids playing together, someone said to me, "This is all your fault." There is certainly truth to that statement. There's no denying I was the catalyst for the family we eventually became, but it wasn't about me. It never was.

People came into our lives because we were open to it. We welcomed anyone who needed a place to call home. Some moved on when they were ready, and others stayed because they belonged.

When Vu asked "what if," I realized that every member of our family had come into our lives for one reason or another. They were meant to be there. We had opened our hearts and our home and let the chips fall where they may.

Most days, it was easy to get caught up in the hustle and bustle of daily activity, but when one of us stopped to wonder "what if," it gave us all pause, a time to reflect on the family unit we had created together.

When I first became a grandmother, I wasn't sure how to feel. I certainly wasn't interested in a sedentary life of leisure. The fact is I have no retirement skills. My entire life has been a series of challenges that I've taken on with unbridled enthusiasm. It wasn't carefully planned out, and it probably wouldn't have worked out if it had been.

Being fired from teaching public school allowed me to follow the road less traveled and led me on a journey of living and loving that I couldn't stop now if I wanted to. That's a good thing because I don't know *how* to retire. It's my nature to pursue things that interest me. That's how I learn and challenge myself, how I channel my energy and curiosity.

I'm not sure how my grandchildren see me, and I know it will be years before they understand many of the things I've done and the choices I've made. Maybe they never will, and that's just fine.

One of the things I noticed as my children got older was that they would use some of the terms and phrases that I had used when raising them, but they would put their own spin on it. It felt good to know that my parenting style had made an impression, even if there were times when they turned my probing questions back on me. I didn't mind that at all. Even more surprising, these days I hear them echo my words to their own children as they navigate their parenting journey. It's comforting to know that some of our parenting styles and family traditions have traveled to another generation.

Ultimately, no matter how they parent or what they do in life, what I do hope is that they realize how fortunate they are to be a member of a family built on happenstance.

Baggage by Holly Werth

"In the end, I am keenly aware it's not a blame game or a victim's paradise. It's a journey that is as innocent as it is universal. A collective effort to find home fueled by a profound need to connect, to connect with each other no matter what our past. I try to repeat those sentiments as I weed through my life with both mothers and now, as a mother myself. Through all the   radiance and darkness, I must remind myself that in the end, no matter my grief or shortcomings, I am here, and I am loved."

– HOLLY MARGOLIES WERTH

MY HUSBAND DOUG has been to Vietnam twice. The first trip was merely out of curiosity. The second became an obsession. He is determined to find my past and all the players who claim to have (or not have) a hand in my upbringing. One of his leads takes him to the orphanage where I spent five months prior to my flight to the States. He manages to track down the caretakers' daily logs from those five months. These diaries document their frustrations and joys of my stubbornness and verve. There are entries of 'she's very loud; she talks too much; Ho Thi is very funny; what a happy and social child' (This cracks me up. Who else could find an orphanage a 'happy' and 'social' place but perhaps a child?) At any rate, not much has changed in forty

231

years. I am still incredibly loud and talk way too much. I'm also gregarious and, at times, funny. It's a stretch to blame or credit these traits on adoption when they already existed way before the 'tragedy of loss' occurred. On the flip side, it's easy to blame my horrid adolescent years on adoption because no "normal" child would be so explosive.

I have a photo of me with my adoptive mother, Marjorie. We are both in Sunday's best and I am carrying a wicker brief-case in one hand while my mother holds my other hand. Why am I carrying a briefcase? Am I going to work? My mom clarifies that it was not work related, but Holly related. Apparently, for many years after my adoption, I was never without this large and rather ugly wicker briefcase. It is filled with everything miscellaneous—mine or stolen. There are items from clean underwear to crackers to playing cards; everything I deem valuable. Children have security blankets and no doubt this was mine. A security 'blanket' carrying everything I need should everything I have disappear. I love this photo.

My post-Vietnam years are littered, to this day, with odd 'packing' behavior. I'm not a hoarder. On the contrary, I am notorious for throwing out things I deem expired even if there is much life left. I'm certain my children will become packrats due to the stress of watching their mom throw out their things. They cannot comprehend why we are unable to keep every doodle masterpiece or flannel onesie from birth until now. My rational explanation usually incites tantrums, so I now resort to 'don't ask, don't tell' middle of the night purging. I can't stand clutter.

Food is another story. The first time my mother-in-law took Doug and me out to a fancy restaurant, she stared in amazement as I ordered. It had nothing to do with the fanciness of the menu; I do the same thing at McDonald's. I can't ex-plain it; my biology takes over and I start to stockpile. Internally I am stressed that there won't be enough to eat so I order for two or three appetites. After witnessing several episodes, my husband has conceded he can't stop this behavior, so he's learned to compensate. To this day, whenever and wherever we eat out, Doug always orders the same thing, 'Ah yeah, I'll just have a glass of water.' Bless his lovely heart. This is a humorous malfunction that may or may not be a consequence of Vietnam. The other malfunctions have little humor to them and are definitely Vietnam.

My mother always says to me 'Holly, your very strength will be your downfall. You are your greatest enemy.' When I push for clarification, she obliges. 'One of the reasons you survived Vietnam was because of your steadfast nature to not only protect but to excel. The very characteristics that kept you alive during the war are grossly out of context here and now.' But the distinction is gray to me. How do you tell an alligator not to snap or a babe not to cry or your husband not to piss all over the toilet seat? You're going up against hardwired behavior. I'm not sure I can control my 'flight or fight' instincts to include certain factors while excluding others. I am specifically talking about my enormous propensity to deceive and hide. My husband often complains that I will take a perfectly good story with hilarious true details and insert hyperbole to heighten the drama even when none is needed. It's so automatic that I don't even know that I'm doing it. There is this primal fear that if I don't deliver, if I fail to wow them, they will leave.

I have this one very old memory of my years in New York shortly after my adoption. There is a boy I have a huge crush on. He invites me over to dinner with his parents. We are eating at the table and talking. They are impressed that my mother has adopted me from Vietnam and want to know all about my life. I cannot recall my full answer, but I do remember portions of it. At one point I tell them that I am on a boat and a helicopter comes by to pick up the children but there's only one problem. Only the children who can climb up the moving ladder can board the helicopter. I am the only one brave enough and proceed to climb mid-air into the cockpit. The boy looks at his father and says, 'That can't be true, can it? Do you believe her, Dad?' I will never forget his answer, 'I believe that she believes it.' He serves me a protective smile and I am grateful for his warmth.

My adult years brought some relief to these lies. When it comes to matters of official importance such as work or friendship or family, I shoot straight. I am ultra-aware of my weakness to spin so I go out of my way to document the facts. While I'm stellar at honest conversations of business and daily life, I find it nearly impossible to voice my true feelings to others especially if these sentiments show any weakness or need. I am unable to process hurt so my workaround is to block it completely.

It's interesting running into friends from the past. Uniformly they tell me I was one tough cookie who didn't need the accolades of anyone, who marched to her own beat. They were drawn to my self-confidence. These remarks secretly floor me because such ambivalence and strength belie the exhaustive energy I spent seeking approval and acceptance. The tales I would spin to catch their envy and bolster my stock. Regardless, I truly am a very tough cookie. I am well aware of the psychobabble of trusting and loving and the healing powers of interdependence. I completely and academically concur. But you know the old fable of the scorpion and the frog? My nature is to protect a six-year-old girl from a world filled with pain and uncertainties. I am the only one she trusts. Sustaining this shield entails a tremendous cost that I don't fully understand but will blindly ante up—I fear until my last breath. And Mom, please remember you lived up to your part of the bargain. I love you.

My Unique Family by Sebastian Pham

I WANTED TO CLOSE THIS BOOK the same way I started it, with a few words from 13-year old Sebastian, a gifted writer and proud member of the family we lovingly call the Pham-inators.

Being part of my unique family, I have had so many cool experiences, some that will stay with me forever. I will always remember one particular experience that happened at the birthday party of one of my many cousins when I was 10 years old. I was able to sit down and converse with author William Jefferson Clinton about the book he had written with James Patterson. I had just read the book, and by just listening to a few sentences coming out of the author's mouth one could tell that he was an extremely well-read and sophisticated person. During our conversation, he explained to me the importance of cyber-security and how our country is vulnerable because of our lack of it. Although our conversation only lasted for about half an hour while my little cousin's birthday party was going on in the background, the depth and sophistication of his speech was amazing, and he was able to explain so much in such a short amount of time.

[After this happened, Bill came over to me and said, "This is what the people currently in the White House don't understand. This is what immigration is all about!"]

At the time, I had never thought about the origins of my family's beginnings in America. My father first set foot in this country after fleeing his own in a boat. Now, here I was sitting across from a former president who was casually talking to me while enjoying his granddaughter's birthday party. How did I get here?

At the age of four, my father and grandmother escaped by sea from Vietnam to the Malaysian refugee camp of Pulau Bidong, which later became a UN refugee camp. My grandmother paid twelve Troy ounces of gold to Chinese smugglers for "safe" passage to Malaysia—although the journey was anything but that. Their boat was raided by Thai pirates who ruthlessly stole anything of value and kidnapped young girls during those three days. During one pirate raid, my young father was crying too loudly, so the captain, to avoid being caught, gave my grandmother a tranquilizer to silence my father. The amount of the lethal elixir was probably enough to kill a creature much larger than my dad, but my grandmother made one of many small decisions that severely affected the future and refused to sentence her son to that fate but at the cost of almost getting caught by pirates.

Upon reaching the shore, my grandmother turned her head to see her cousin weeping over the body of her four-year-old son, who had drowned during the swim onto the beach, but this does not even compare to what happened to less fortunate families. Imagine losing your entire family while trying to give them a better life, on top of fleeing the country your family has called home for generations. This was the unfortunate fate of many refugees. The loss that my grandmother's cousin took was great, but the fate they suffered was almost lucky compared to the fate of many others.

Six grueling months were spent at the Pulau Bidong Refugee Camp until the Lutheran Refugee Service placed my father and grandmother with an American sponsor family. While at the camp, my dad's cousins would use my dad, a cute little four-year-old, to ask for milk or food from soldiers on the island, for their rations were meager. Another story my grandma would always tell was about the time my dad had an abscess on his forehead, and because there were no doctors on the island, they had to cut the abscess with a razor. My grandmother vividly described how my dad was horrified as he watched them take the razor, which had been sterilized in boiled seawater over a campfire and hold him down so they could terminate the infection.

Had the folder that belonged to my father and grandmother landed on another social worker's desk, then I would not be a part of the unique family that I am a part of today. What would have happened if that social worker called in sick, or if my American grandma was not home to take the call that led to her sponsoring my father? Had my biological grandmother missed the boat to Malaysia, or was short one ounce of gold, my dad could be selling newspapers on the streets of Vietnam right now.

Sitting there talking to a former president made me realize how different things could have been if we hadn't had fortune on our side, or if my American grandma had made a different decision.

Half of this story boils down to luck. It just happened that my grandmother made it to the boat on time, had enough gold, and their file did end up landing on that case worker's desk who didn't call in sick that day. My American grandma was home to take the call and sponsor my dad. I ask myself:

What does this all mean? Why isn't my dad on the streets of Saigon selling newspapers? Why am I sitting here writing this? What am I supposed to do with this luck that myself and my family were blessed with? *I may never find the answer to these questions.*

The other half of my story boils down to our actions and the ripple effect it has on the people around us. If not for the goodwill and decency of people making the right decisions and actions, this world would be a terrible and chaotic place to live. If not for my American grandma accepting my dad and biological grandmother into her home without a second thought, I would not be here. Although the phrases 'make the right decision' and 'be a good person' may be cliché, they are still phrases we must follow. Common decency and our actions are the anchors that hold our world to the bottom, keeping us from drifting away toward chaos and evil. Sometimes there may not be a 'right decision,' but if every day we keep making good decisions that we think are 'right,' we can make the world a better place and help others either unintentionally or intentionally. It doesn't need to be adopting or sponsoring countless refugees as my American grandma did, but if we start small we can help so many people.

All of these factors of luck and actions came together at the right time to put me here writing this. Even though I was able to have my family, some were not as lucky. The child of my grandma's cousin, who had aspirated too much seawater. The young girls, kidnapped by pirates. The hundreds of refugees who didn't get sponsored so quickly or the refugees that starved to death on that island.

Why was I put here, why did my dad survive the journey, not those young girls that were kidnapped by pirates, or my grandmother's cousin's son? Since my family was fortunate enough, what am I supposed to do about it? If I can make the right decisions myself, who knows what the ripple effect could be, how many people I can help. Maybe that is the meaning of this, why I was put here, to let people have the fortune that I had, the fortune that put me here today and put me with my unique family.

Acknowledgments

THANK YOU to everyone who contributed to this project including:
Callista Chimombo
Diane Cirincione
Susan Cox
David Eisenhower
Ronni Ginott
Arlene Halpern
Chuck Henschel
Joe Kennedy II
Irene Lane
Allen Litvin
Brynn MacDougall
Lee Heh Margolies
Andrew Mezvinsky
Marc Mezvinsky
Kathy Nelson
Susan Nickelson
Sebastian Pham
Vu Pham
Amy Pham
Lilly Price
Sue Rubell
Dave Smitherman
David Sostman
Sofia Tamimi
Marna Tucker
Doug Werth
And of course, Holly Margolies Werth.
With a special thanks to Dave Smitherman.

I am so appreciative of my family and friends for helping me try to accurately piece together the past few decades of my unconventional life. To anyone whom I may have omitted, please understand that the oversight is a direct result of the whirlwind of information circling around in my brain and not a reflection on the importance of your contribution or support. I remain eternally grateful to all of you.

The Author

MARJORIE MARGOLIES is a former member of Congress from Pennsylvania, a journalist, a women's rights advocate, and a serendipitous mother many times over. She is perhaps best remembered for being the first unmarried American to adopt a foreign child and for casting the deciding vote in favor of President Clinton's 1993 budget, the Omnibus Reconciliation Act.

Born in Philadelphia, Margolies graduated from the University of Pennsylvania. She worked as a journalist with NBC and its owned and operated stations for 25 years, winning five Emmy Awards.

Running as a Democrat, she was elected to represent the traditionally Republican 13th District of Pennsylvania in Congress. She was also the deputy chair of the United States delegation to the United Nations Fourth World Conference for Women in Beijing in 1995. As a result of that experience, she founded Women's Campaign International (WCI), an organization that provides empowerment training for women around the world.

She is currently a faculty member at the Annenberg School of Communication at the University of Pennsylvania, and at last count, her family consisted of 11 children and 21 grandchildren.

≈

View the author's photo collection at
MarjorieMargolies.com.

Ingram Content Group UK Ltd.
Milton Keynes UK
UKHW042336030523
421181UK00001B/49

9 781954 332294